JUST MY LUCK

◆

A Humorous Account
Of Life's Absurdities

KYLE WOODRUFF

"Your ability to find the silly in the serious will take you far."

—Fortune cookie from

a mediocre Chinese restaurant

(Lucky Numbers: 14, 7, 30, 22, 5, 27)

For Esther,

who always believed in and encouraged my writing.

R.I.P.

CONTENTS

PREFACE

Just My Luck outlines several stories illustrating a track record of bad luck in my life. I've often reached for an explanation, wondering if I'm carrying some kind of karmic baggage from a past incarnation. (I once expressed that notion to my boss after a series of deals fell through, saying that I must have been part of Genghis Khan's troop of marauders to deserve such misfortune. He consoled me by saying, "What a surprise. You were a piece of shit back then and you're a piece of shit now!") Recently, however, I may have found an explanation for my bad luck in this current lifetime.

My father was an aerospace engineer for more than thirty-five years at a well-established parachute manufacturer. He worked on projects such as designing aerodynamic decelerators for the military, as well as NASA missions that landed rovers on Mars. Somewhere amidst his career, his team bid for a job against their competitors to work with a company we'll call ABC. My father's competition won the bid and began manufacturing parachutes for a big ABC project. However, before the project launched, ABC went belly-up, leaving their partners holding the bill—a huge financial loss.

Years later, a company similar to ABC came around, proposing a similarly ambitious project. This time, my father's company won the bid. However, their new partner insisted that my father's company pay for the test drops, a fee that was typically covered by the purchasing company ever since the

ABC incident happened. During the negotiations, my father asked the CEO, "How do we know this won't be another case of ABC?"

"How *dare* you compare us to ABC!" the CEO barked out over the phone.

My father shared this story over Thanksgiving dinner one year, and when he revealed that the company he was negotiating with was SpaceX, I nearly dropped my forkful of mashed potatoes.

"You *personally* insulted Elon Musk?" I asked.

"Yup!" my father said with a sense of glee. "But this was long before he became the *second* richest man in the world." The word "second" was spat out as if anyone short of first was just another loser in his book.

I wondered what Elon was doing at that exact moment as I pushed around my peas. Was he telling the inverse of that same story to his own family at Thanksgiving?

"And then he compared us to ABC!" Elon would recall, enraged. "So, you know what I did just to spite the bastard? Just before I launched that Tesla into space, I carved a nice little message into the hood of the vehicle that read, 'Fuck the Woodruffs!'"

And so, it all makes sense now, my bad luck. My father insulted the man with the most potential to save humanity from obliteration, once he's colonized Mars and Earth gets hit by an asteroid or whatever. A certain degree of karma must come from your family name floating around the heavens in shame, carved by the future savior of humanity.

The best part is that years after telling this story, SpaceX actually purchased my father's company. My father had already retired by that time, but part of me likes to think it was Elon's plan to fire Mr. Woodruff and destine his children to starve.

FOREWARNING

I just wanted to give you a heads up about things in here that could possibly be triggering. Let's kick the list off with the classics, shall we? There's mention of drugs, guns, alcohol, and sex. There's foul language and name calling. There's speeding and law breaking. There are penises and policemen and prostitutes and poop. There are references to forbidden words, like "r*tard" and "f*ggot" (except I don't put an asterisk in the middle as we pretend like I'm not really saying them when we both know I am). There's nudity, and a black man, both in the same story. There is talk of revenge and even jokes about hitting children. There is a boat, in a moat, with a goat, in a coat. And if you do not like green eggs and ham, I'd turn back now, my fellow Sam.

Actually, there are no boats, moats, or goats. But if you're so sensitive that making fun of any one of these things may upset you, I suggest leaving this book where you found it. If you're so fragile that reading a single bad word is enough to ruffle your feathers, I would just use this book as kindling instead of reading it. If you're so woke that any one of these things may send you into a tizzy, I would just throw this book in the trash and cancel me on Twitter now. (In fact, let me save you the trouble and pre-cancel myself.) So, if you get to the end of this book after being forewarned and you're looking for an apology, well, don't hold your breath. Or on second thought, maybe do.

BEACH-CATION

"Some family trees
bear an enormous crop of nuts."
—Wayne Huizenga

For nearly two decades—from the time I was in diapers to the time of legal drinking age—my extended family took an annual week-long vacation at the beach every summer. Somewhere in my early years of babbling, I deemed this our "beach-cation," and the term stuck around. Being locked in a cottage with kooky relatives created some of the best memories of my life, reemerging anytime I smell sunscreen.

Our family was considered large compared to some. My father had three brothers who had wives who had children. There were nine of us ankle-grabbers—seven boys and two girls—spawned over the course of thirteen years. Due to the volume of children, every father drove a minivan out of necessity. On the first morning of beach-cation, each father would Tetris his way into a jam-packed van full of suitcases, duffle bags, coolers, boogie boards, fishing gear, toys, and whatever else families might need—like booze. Then they'd meet at a commuter lot and perform a child swap so the girls could pair up and the boys could ride with boys their own age.

In the early years, we'd drive ninety minutes from central Connecticut to Misquamicut, Rhode Island; in the later years, we'd make the few-hour trek to Long Beach Island, New Jersey. Either way, at those respective ages, it felt like an eternity. There were the original Game Boys back then, but you could only stare into that tiny little screen for so long before your eyes began to bleed. Besides, you were so excited to see your cousins that the goofing off would begin immediately and our parents would be locked in chaos until we arrived.

There was giggling and arguing and "Are we there yet?"s and banana peels tossed around. Once an untimely moth fluttered into the window as we were over a traffic-filled bridge. My poor old bridge-o-phobic grandma was white-knuckling the dashboard as it was when my sister belted out a blood-curdling scream. Grandma yelled out a scream of her own as she thought the bridge was collapsing. When she realized it wasn't, she clutched her heart and turned around to say, "What!?"

"I don't know," said my sister calmly, the moth fluttering out the window again, "a bug or something."

Grandma gave her a lecture about the delicacy of an old lady's heart as the rest of us snickered in the background.

Eventually we'd arrive for the annual stop at our favorite breakfast diner. Soon after we'd placed our orders, some of the boys would play a game the girls weren't dumb enough to be roped into. It was called "Sugar or Salt" and involved a blind taste test of a spoonful of white powder. It wasn't much of a *game*, per se, for two reasons: 1) because the answer was immediate as soon as the victim put the spoon in their mouth, and 2) because it was usually salt. But to extinguish the boredom of childhood back then, you had to rely on this archaic thing called "your imagination."

Over breakfast we asked the passengers from the other vans what happened in their cars on the drive. One year, my cousin reported that my father got so impatient with traffic that he decided to veer off the road, down a hill, and across a grassy median into a parallel lane of traffic.

"Wow!" I said. "Did it work?"

"Nah," my cousin shook his head with a sigh. "Traffic turned out even worse over there."

Sunny days on the beach were obviously the highlight of beach-cation. Sometime in youth—after testosterone started pumping, but before underaged drinking clouded innocence—a game called "Trust" emerged. The game was played at the peak of high tide when there was a rapid swell of crashing waves flowing to shore. There were two cousins and one inner tube involved in Trust—a pushee, who sat with their back to the oncoming waves, and a pusher, who faced the swell and steered the tube.

The pushee's hope was that their pilot could navigate them safely into the calm waters beyond the break, but of course, that never happened. You knew darn well that when you were the pusher blindly guiding someone in your care, firing off a last-second "*Oops!*" as you shoved them into a wave was far too tempting. But that was the unspoken understanding of Trust: sometimes you were the butcher, and others you were the lamb.

This was one of those boyhood games that usually involved someone getting hurt just enough to be funny, but not enough to warrant a trip to the hospital. You know, *nearly* drowning was great, but *actually* drowning would have been a downer. At least that's how you felt with a view of oncoming waves when in control over someone else's fate. But when you were sitting in the tube yourself, abiding by the only rule of Trust—"You're not allowed to look!"—there was only anxious anticipation for the moment your throne went roller coasting into the receding surf, and you gulped down a bunch of water. I can recall knocking my chin on the ocean floor and chipping a tooth or having the wind knocked out of me while tumbling under the force of waves. But as most stupid and indestructible boys do, we bounced right back for more.

Creations like these highlight the cloth from which I'm cut, the seed from which I'm sown. That is to say, my gene pool is filled with nonsense and stupidity. My adolescent father and uncles would do things like shoot a bow and arrow straight into the backyard sky, then run away as fast as their little legs would carry them. They only realized this might be unwise when after sprinting for cover in the nearby shed and one arrow came piercing down through the old rooftop and stuck in the ground between their feet. That didn't discourage them from abusing Lawn Darts, though (an outdoor game played by throwing fletched, footlong metal rods at targets, banned in the 1980s after a few skull punctures caused brain injuries and untimely deaths). An annual game that surfaced every fall for them involved throwing crab apples at each other's heads for no reason. Again, let me emphasize the importance of no hospital trips, but any bruises, black eyes, or concussions were fair game, even welcomed.

Who birthed these maniacs, you wonder? That would have been my grandmother, whose tolerance for this kind of behavior I'd like to highlight now.

One winter evening, the boys were sledding down the long hill in the field behind their house when the dinner bell rang. "We'll be right in!" they called. "Just one more run!" But, as legend has it, the sledding was too good for just one more run. They got greedy and kept sledding for another twenty minutes as dinner got cold. When they finally marched up the back steps, exhausted from the thrill, Mom was waiting in the doorway with her arms crossed and steam rising from her ears.

"If you little *brats*," she yelled, grabbing the first one by the scruff of his neck and the belt of his snowsuit and heaving him across the kitchen floor, "*ever* let dinner get that cold again," she said as the first slid into the opposite wall and banged his head and the next brother came flying toward him, "I'll wring your *necks*," she added as the third brother was tossed onto the pile, "and serve *you* for dinner," she finished as the fourth brother landed on top of them. Keep in mind this woman grew up during the Great Depression, where her family was so desperate for food at times that her father stewed squirrel just to put a meal on the table. Lessons in gratitude were instilled in a different way during her parental heyday.

By the time us grandchildren were that old, though, Grandma's strictness had long since worn down from rearing four hooligans. She was still strict, of course, but old and sweet, calmer and fair. When it came to encouraging good behavior in the youth, she had adopted a positive reward system as opposed to the aforementioned negative one.

"Gummy worms are only awarded to *good* boys and girls!" she'd announce at the start of beach-cation, dangling her infamous bag of treats in the air. "Do I have any of those here?"

"Me! Me! Me!" the cries would ensue all around.

"We'll just see about *that!*" she'd say. But it was always a bluff; the coveted gummies were never withheld. I think the girls usually got theirs first, then it was either oldest to youngest, or youngest to oldest. Or maybe she went in order of birthdays, or reverse order of birthdays. Or maybe she mixed up the order entirely. She did whatever she could to make it seem random, never to hint at her favorite. (And although some cousins might argue, I know it was me.)

Boogie boarding was always a thrill on beach-cation, especially once we got old enough to fight stronger tides. Once I got caught in a rip current so bad that I almost got swept out to sea. I paddled my heart out just to stay within sight of the shore as I was carried a quarter mile down to the next lifeguard chair. I finally landed on the beach and sprawled out with my heart racing as the man in red trunks stood over me asking if I was okay. He claimed he had an eye on me, that he would've jumped in if he thought I might drown. "Thanks a lot," I said, thinking those shots of tequila and the bowl I'd smoked right beforehand were a bad idea.

The problem with vacation is, it's always a good time to have a drink or get a little high. The role models I looked up to all throughout youth already had a Bloody Mary in their hands by the time I woke up in the morning. I'd be slurping down a bowl of cereal around 10AM and they'd be shuffling off for an "afternoon" nap. Granted they'd been up since five, playing tennis or going for sunrise walks down the beach, but at that point of my waking consciousness, all I witnessed was the morning cocktails. It was easy to follow in those footsteps by the time our oldest cousins figured out how to smuggle booze into their suitcases.

By the time we were old enough to drive, one of my cousins decided to bring his Jeep down to the Jersey Shore. We rolled a joint and took a little top-down cruise up the main boulevard. Halfway through the ride, a cop pulled up behind us and decided we were going a bit too fast for his liking, so he threw on the red and blue. As a marine going into the service after the summer, it wouldn't have been a good look for my cousin, so he did the heroic thing and swallowed the rest of the joint whole. After he flashed his marine ID, though, we were off the hook and zoomed back to the cottage to satisfy our munchies.

Lunches on beach-cation, boy, those were to drool over. By the time we were old enough to scrounge through the cabinets, we were basically on our own. The menu at that age often consisted of a healthy slather of jelly and cream cheese on a hot dog roll, washed down with an ice-cold root beer and maybe a handful (or bag) of marshmallows for dessert—something I now refer to as The Diabetes Platter. In later years, we often fished for our meals, pulling in striper or scup right off the shore. Or maybe we'd rake clams from the salt pond, cooking them up with farm-grown corn and veggies on the charcoal grill. *Mmm-mm!* There's nothing like harvesting your own meal from the earth around you and chomping it down under the sun with a cold summer beer.

At least once per vacation the family would treat us to a big lobster dinner. We'd buy 'em live, steam 'em in pots, cracked 'em open, then dip 'em in butter and kick 'em down with other fixings to our hearts' delight. The first year I got a taste of lobster was one of the earlier years I remember. The lobsters were "bad" that year, whatever that means (somehow not up to our parents' standards), so they were shelled out to us, and we ate until we had our fill. I had no prior lobster to compare it to, so anything at that age slathered in butter was delicious. Pretty sure we begged for some the next year, and the meal turned from an adult-only party to an all-inclusive tradition.

On rainy days on beach-cation (which I recall thinking were a total injustice), we'd stay inside and play games. In a time before Wi-Fi and smartphones, entertainment came in the form of board games, card games, and crossword puzzles. For some reason, the background music for these memories is always "Take Me To The River" by the Talking Heads. Well, it's not "for some reason"; it's because the cottage in those days had that mounted largemouth bass that would flop around and sing whenever you pushed the little button. So now the words *Drop me in the water!* are etched into my brain forever because some annoying kid or another kept pushing that damn button. (It was me. I was obsessed with that bass.)

I can also remember an impressive stack of VHS tapes we worked through year after year before they went extinct. Most of them were adult-rated films like *Anaconda*, *Towering Inferno*, or *Terminator*. I can certainly recall watching *Cujo* at too young an age, so thanks to whatever parent let that happen. I'm guessing all the television is part of what kept us kids wired throughout the nighttime because I don't recall doing much sleeping on beach-cation. I think our parents took a hiatus from setting bedtimes because I remember doing front flips off of barstools to body slam cousins on couches into the wee hours of the morning. It's a good thing no one rolled off and smashed their head on the glass coffee table two feet away. That hospital trip would have put the kibosh on that evening ritual.

When we were young, entertainment came in the form of running around pretending to be *Transformers*, roping unsuspecting victims into our game. "Get 'em!" the boys would yell at the girls, followed by the sounds of imaginary laser blasters: *Pew! Pew! Pew! Pew! Pew! Pew!*

The girls didn't much care for that game, but it was their fault for being outnumbered. By the time we were older, entertainment came in the form of a week-long buzz. One memory that stands out was playing "Snapple-and-Tequila Pong," which is as terrible of an idea as it sounds. Another was "Surprise Pong," named for the six different shots of liquor filched from our parents' supply and poured into different Solo cups. (Don't worry, we did the courteous thing and topped off the bottles with water so they'd never know the difference. But

I think karma came as the kind of hangover you'd imagine comes from mixing so many liquors.) Yet another memory was of hotboxing the outdoor shower, six of us crammed into an oxygen-deprived space, passing around joints. Those kinds of antics might have resulted in someone streaking around the block that night. Or maybe we'd empty a bunch of firecrackers into a beach shell on the balcony and light up the whole street with gunpowder as if it were broad daylight. We didn't burn down the cottage that year per se, but we did melt the picnic table and lost Grandma's security deposit.

The fondest memory of beach-cation was innocent enough, though. On the last night, we'd make sure to walk that mile down the beach to *Dusty's* ice cream. There, we'd each get an oversized glob of dairy goodness that was sure to go dripping down your arm. In my opinion, it was the best way to wrap up those week-long memories.

SANTA'S REVENGE

"No, I'm an accountant.
I wear this f*cking thing
as a fashion statement, alright?"
—Willie from Bad Santa

Growing up, my cousin Dan had a bald spot on the back of his head. It was caused by the same thing that gave my uncle's wrist arthritis, although it was nothing genetic. It came from often receiving what my uncle deemed a SUTH, or "slap upside the head," for constant misbehavior. There are some people in this world who require that kind of constant feedback to course-correct their path in life. And if anyone I know deserved such a bald spot, it was surely Max, the latchkey bully.

In the late nineties, I attended an after-school program where kids whose parents worked late were supervised by what can only be classified as glorified babysitters. One such supervisor was named Judy. Or maybe it was Jody. I don't really remember. But the point is, one day I was sitting across from Judy/Jody, talking about the upcoming holiday season.

"So, what did you ask Santa to bring you for Christmas?" she asked.

"*Welll*," I began excitedly.

That's when a voice appeared from behind me. "You still believe in *Santa!?*"

Excuse me? I thought, turning to find an eye-level finger digging through a belly button that was protruding from under a plain white tee. It belonged to Max, standing with his pale tummy so close to my face that I could smell what he'd been digging for.

Somewhere along the line, Max's parents had failed him. He had been free to run rampant, mouthing off far too often without a good SUTH. Max had the tendency to go up to any unsuspecting victim, student or teacher, and slam his arms across his crotch in the formation of an X. Then they would explode off his thighs as he yelled, "Suck it!" His second favorite gesture was to loosely pound one wrist across his chest and say, "What are you, *retarded!?*" This was often directed at some poor kid just because he wore glasses. Where a child at this tender age had learned such things was beyond me, but it was a habit that would never be broken.

"Max!" yelled Judy, frowning in a way I didn't realize then meant, "Ixnay on the Antasay."

What's going on? I wondered, seeing Jody's expression. *Of course I believe in Santa! Everyone believes in Santa. Who else delivers all the toys to children across the worl—*

"What are you, retarded!?" These were the next words to emerge from Max's fat head, his expression scrunched in contempt as if I'd just asked if the sky was green and the grass blue.

"*Max!*" yelled Judy-Jody. "Let him *believe* what he wants to believe."

Why did she say "believe" like that? I wondered.

"It's okay," said Jody, turning to console me. "Santa's still real."

What do you mean "still"? I thought. *As if there was ever a doubt!*

"Pfft," Max spat out, rolling his eyes. As he turned to leave, he just audibly muttered, "Stupid…"

"*Max!*" yelled Judy once more.

"Suck it!" yelled Max as he jiggled away.

"Sorry about that," said Jody. "You were saying?"

"I was saying"..? I thought, staring at her blankly. *What's going on around here? What are you guys talking about? And how is Max allowed to tell adults to "Suck it!" without getting his head bashed in?*

Suddenly Ju-Jody was called to help with another supervisor. So there I was, recently diagnosed with mental retardation, questioning my grip on reality.

What happens to all the milk and cookies? And the carrots! Surely the carrots are consumed by reindeer. Dasher? Prancer? I know Santa's real; I sat on his lap at the mall last week!

I struggled to wrap my head around their disbelief, but that year I was thrown a loop when my parents got divorced. Because of this, Christmas took place in two different households, and upon close examination, it appeared that "Santa" delivered gifts with two different handwritings.

Last Christmas, I thought about Max, wondering where life had taken him. I figured he'd gone one of two ways: He was either A) wearing a suit and tie somewhere on Wall Street, or B) living above a dingy strip club, eating greasy Chinese takeout five nights a week. One would hope it's the former, but even then, I'd suspect he'd have a dark side, lingering a little too close to playgrounds or what have you.

A long time had passed before I searched for him. The first link that appeared was titled "Prisoner Gets Loose, Crashes Police Cruiser," and I immediately thought, *Now we're talking!* I clicked, and it led me to a video with this description:

A state trooper was transporting a prisoner to the [City] Correctional Center in the passenger seat of a Police cruiser Friday, when the prisoner freed himself from his handcuffs, assaulted the trooper, and forced the vehicle to crash.

The video began with images of a smashed-up cruiser being towed away, and a reporter picking up the story with something like, "Well, this isn't your typical fender bender, Bob." That's when the video flashed to a report showing the arrest took place two towns from our school, with a birthdate close to mine, confirming I'd found my guy.

After interviewing a witness who described the car bouncing from one jersey barrier to the next, the reporter mentioned that as they crashed, "[The prisoner] got out of the cruiser and ran down the embankment, fleeing to some nearby woods."

The word "fleeing" triggered a flashback of playing dodgeball with Max. He wasn't much of a "runner," per se; more of a waddler at best, and even that's a generous term of locomotion. He certainly wasn't doing much "fleeing" from the balls us skinny kids chucked at his head when everyone aimed for the easy target. Always a graceful loser, though, Max would chop that X across his groin and yell, "Suck it!" loud enough for the entire gym to hear.

"[City] police caught up with him a short time later," the reporter continued. No surprise there, but when the video cut back to the witness saying, "It was pretty unbelievable," I couldn't help but think the *most* unbelievable part was the fact that Max slipped those handcuffs over his fat wrists.

On top of the original charges, Max faced new charges such as "Escape," "Assaulting an officer," "Interfering with an investigation," and "Loosely pounding one wrist at the officers who tried to subdue him." I might have made that last one up, but I'm sure he considered it once he learned about his $100,000 bail.

I was curious to find out what happened, so I investigated further. It didn't take long to find his inmate number and arrest details on PublicPoliceRecords.com. Turns out he's in the middle of serving an eight-year sentence in a correctional institute that ironically I'd driven by countless times when I worked nearby.

I also searched his inmate number to see if I could find a photo. Sure enough, there he was: arms crossed, leaning back on what may have been the same brick wall we did during foursquare. He was still wearing that plain white tee. I guess some things never change. But what had changed was the fact that he was now wearing thick, black-framed glasses. They were the same pair he used to tease that other kid for back in the day, and I couldn't help thinking, *Who's the retard now?*

When I clicked on the photo to make it larger, I was brought to a website called LoveAPrisoner.com. It appeared to be some kind of Match.com for convicts with a dating profile. Under his photo was a description of his characteristics, his incarceration and release dates, and information so his future lover would know exactly what he was in jail for: ASSAULT, ESCAPE, DRUGS—the triple crown of date-ability.

The best part was the screenshot of a hand written note:

Hello, my name is Max. I like to joke around and have a good time. I'm looking for a friend to write to, in and hopefully outside of prison. I have many aspirations for when I'm released and take this incarceration as a learning experience. I have my own money and will never ask for any. So if you wish to know more, please write me.

Casting a bottled letter into the vast dating ocean like this seemed as likely to get a reply as sending a gift list to The North Pole, but at least he's not a gold digger.

I suppose after all these years I should feel sympathy for the guy—perhaps wondering where things went wrong, about how latchkey had failed him, about whether or not I could have done something had I only searched for him sooner—but instead, all I could think about was trolling him with anonymous love letters for the next couple of years using the pen name "Believe In Me." Then, when the time came to meet upon his release, I would do something long overdue: Show up dressed as Santa and deliver a well-deserved SUTH.

BOYS

"A boy is Truth with dirt on its face,
Beauty with a cut on its finger,
Wisdom with bubble gum in its hair,
and the Hope of the future
with a frog in its pocket."
—Unknown

What started out as innocent play on a dreamy childhood afternoon turned into an absolute nightmare I wouldn't wish upon my worst enemy.

My neighborhood friend Ken and I rode our bikes to the park one summer and hopped on the swings. As things often do with adolescent boys, this turned into a testosterone-fueled competition. It was a race to see who could swing the highest, and when it appeared we were evenly matched, Ken decided to step things up a notch. While at opposite ends of the pendulum—Ken forward at his peak, me back at mine—Ken was kind enough to spit straight up in the air with a slight angle in hopes that his ball of saliva would collide with his chum upon descent.

Registering a tad late the trap that had been laid out before me, I could do nothing but pray his moistened projectile was poorly timed. Lucky for me, it was. Unfortunately for Ken, I was onto his devilish scheme and returned the favor while on the peak of my own upward swing. Not expecting such a sudden reply, Ken, too, was at the mercy of prayer that the timing of my mucosal missile was misjudged. Lucky for him, it was. At this point, it was an all-out war of senseless pride: Who could land the first spitball on their swinging friend?

Back and forth we went, spitting and recalculating angles, adjusting for shifting wind speeds and swing trajectories. We dialed in closer, missing by mere fractions of an inch or even spattering our rival with the trailing particles of saliva that "didn't count." Then it happened. At the pinnacle of Ken's highest swing, he hocked up the throatiest loogie he could muster. At the right angle, with the proper wind conditions and necessary salivatory volume, I swung with full force into the path of his oral abomination, catching it directly in my mouth.

I lost all focus in disgust and was launched from the apex of my swing. I went flying off onto the woodchip floor and sprained an ankle upon landing. I rolled in a cloud of dust, retching for mercy at what had just occurred. (To this day, I have gag-reflexive PTSD just thinking about the reality of consuming phlegm coughed up by another human being.) Needless to say, I lost.

In a less foul, more idiotic episode of what we deemed "Swing Wars," I learned another important lesson about the dangers of these chain-hung liabilities. The father of our friend Jonathan had bolted a piece of lumber between the trunks of two towering Oaks in their yard, dangling a pair of swings far below for his childhood friends to play. But why settle for that boring tendency to swing parallel to one another, we thought, when you could make things more interesting by swinging *at* one another?

We launched toward each other at full speed, feet extended like jousting poles, each attempting to knock the other to the ground. We enjoyed a brief and thrilling duel, sustaining just a few minor bruises that were brushed off with the boyish laughter that comes from being hurt by one of your friends. Then, with a particularly hard-hitting joust, my buddy struck my feet at just the right angle to send me spinning wildly out of control. The world blurred in circles around me briefly before I went crashing into one of the trees. *Wham!*—the back of my head collided with the gnarly bark, and I was seeing stars. (To this day, I have a flat spot on the back of my skull that I don't recall being there before that moment in time.) Needless to say, I lost.

You'd think we'd have learned our lesson about wars of any kind after those incidents, but boys aren't subdued by the bumps and bruises of life so easily. The thing about enormous Oak trees is, every fall they deposit enormous acorns, and loads of enormous acorns are perfect for throwing at your friends.

In the brisk afternoons of October after school, the neighborhood kids would gather in the very same woods that hosted Swing Wars and agree upon the one and only rule of Acorn Wars: Every man for himself!

Shortly thereafter, Ken, Jonathan, Michael, and I would scatter for cover behind trees, scooping up the largest specimens we could find, hoping not to get pelted from behind on the sprint to cover. Then, an all-out battle would erupt as nuts as hard as rocks would go whizzing through the air.

The every-man-for-himself rule provided an even playing field for all who could throw an object from here to there. Anyone who thought they were fast enough to make a run for cover from one tree to the next when their reachable supply of ammo had been burned, though, was sorely mistaken: a barrage of artillery from all angles was their inescapable fate. But the only other choice was to remain a sitting duck as your enemies made a strategic ploy to surround your sorry ass.

It's amazing the number of direct hits a young boy can endure when pumped full of raging hormones and stupidity. These games would go on until the fleeting sunlight drained from the sky and darkness consumed the last rays of hope in seeing your enemies. Only the next day would you realize how hard you'd been bombarded, counting the bruises on your back, arms, and—if your reflexes had failed you in a flash of crossfire—neck.

One rather unfortunate afternoon, I'd done a mostly decent job of dipping and dodging the ambush of wooden marbles that'd gone zipping by. But in a moment of lackadaisical disregard, a friend grasped an opportunity to sneak up on me and beam an acorn right at my face from close range. By the time I saw it coming it was too late. The pointed tip of the damn thing hit me just above the eyes. I immediately felt a sharp pain and, sure enough, a warm trickle of blood ensued. Needless to say...

I went home to clean up, and when I arrived, it was clear I owed my father an explanation. I shared the rules and purpose of the game the best that you can describe a rule-less game with no purpose. "Sounds dangerous," my father told me in a stoic manner. Then he added, "You could have lost an eye." After thinking for a moment, he stepped into the garage and grabbed a pair of safety glasses, handed them to me, and off I went to enjoy the blissfully ignorant virtues of being a boy.

WRITING ON THE WALL

"Most of us can read the writing on the wall;
we just assume it's addressed to someone else."
—Ivern Ball

Do you ever wonder what happened to those kids you went to grade school with? One rotten apple I'd lost track of over the years was named Erik. When I saw my Facebook friend requests the other day, though, there he was. I had forgotten all about him, but as soon as I scrolled through his photos, it all came rushing back to me.

He was one of those—How do I put this nicely?—short bus kids. Not the physically disabled ones, nor the ones with an "intellectual developmental disorder," or whatever the proper term for mental retardation is these days. No, none of that. Our school just had a small pack of, well, misfits that stuck together on field trips and such. They were just a little weird, or socially awkward, or whatever description you're comfortable with. But I'm sure you know what I mean.

Let me give you a quick example.

The first time the mile run was introduced in gym class, Erik decided a mile was a bit much for his liking. While everyone else followed the instructions of running four laps, Erik chose to run three. When everyone pointed out that Erik had "finished" at the same time, despite being lapped by everyone in class, he firmly denied such a *ridiculous* accusation. When the teacher asked Erik to look him in the eyes and tell him the truth, Erik feigned an asthma attack. That motherfucker didn't have asthma; everyone knew that! But instead of a swift kick in the ass, the teacher sent him to the nurse to lie down and eat crackers—the cure for everything in those days. Erik may think he got away with it, but *I* know his clock is still ticking.

Speaking of ticking clocks, a year or so later Erik carried that same mentality into Middle School, where he once wrote "Tick Tick Boom @ 10 o'clock" on the bathroom wall in hopes of sparing himself the last lap around school that day. Shortly after someone found it, the whole school was shuffled out into a parking lot that the staff, you know, *hoped* was far enough away. Then a bomb squad came to sweep the property. When they discovered nothing, that the threat was empty, they herded us back into the school and proceeded to take attendance.

Would you like to take a wild guess at who was the only one missing?

Erik thought that if he ducked into the woods and ran home when no one was looking, they'd never notice. Lucky for him, his house was less than a mile away. Not so lucky for him, it didn't take a genius to figure out what happened.

The staff confronted Erik about it the next day, saying the handwriting on the wall looked suspiciously like his. And in true Erik fashion, he denied such a *ridiculous* accusation. But when feigning an asthma attack failed him this time, he fessed up.

The principal gave him a real stern talking to, then they suspended him from school for three whole days. Let me rephrase that: *"...then gave him a three-day vacation from what he was trying to avoid in the first place."* Does that sound like punishment to you? Because it sounds like a mission accomplished to me. My guess is that it didn't exactly course-correct his path toward becoming a menace to society.

If I were principal, that little bastard would have spent the next three days scrubbing every bathroom in the school with his toothbrush. *That's* a punishment that might sink in, not being sent home to lie down and eat crackers.

Look, I'm a firm believer that unsolicited child abuse is wrong, but if a kid makes a bomb threat before puberty, one good slap upside the head might not be a bad idea. And before you get in a tizzy about how hitting children is wrong, just let me tell you about who he grew up to be.

Before ignoring his friend request, I flipped through an assortment of photos that can only be described as concerning. Let's start with his profile picture: a blurry selfie wearing a jubilant expression holding up a bag of Tom's Fried Pork Skins. Not my cup of tea, but not the red flags I'm referring to either.

In the second photo, he was wearing a deranged mask of an old man, holding a chainsaw.

"Well surely this was posted on Halloween," you say. And that's true—if we've moved Halloween to May 19th!

The next photo wasn't a photo of Erik at all, but rather a display of knives, viciously stabbed into a table.

In the next, he had a crew cut, wearing some kind of official-looking uniform with a badge and the first thought that sprung to mind was, *Jesus, I hope they don't give this guy a gun!*

In the next, he was wearing a flak jacket and I said, "Jesus, they give this guy a gun!"

Next was a photo of a young Michael Jackson around the time he was in The Jackson 5. The caption of the meme read,

"Nighty night. Keep ya butthole tight," and I yelled out, "They give this guy *a gun!*"

When the next photo showed Erik drunkenly holding up an AR-15, it confirmed what had been the writing on the wall all along.

And look, I'm not suggesting we bring corporal punishment back to schools, but one good smack might've jogged loose whatever wires that were crossed in his brain. No? Just one...

HERO

"I'll be back."
—Arnold Schwarzenegger,
Terminator

Computer labs began to make an appearance in high schools around my sophomore year. I signed up for a class on Microsoft Office taught by some ancient, balding dinosaur. He was a plump sourpuss with thick glasses and poor posture. His monotone delivery was terribly difficult to pay attention to as a teenager, especially amidst a rivalry with your classmate to see who could fling the most pencils into the ceiling or play the loudest clip from an Arnold Schwarzenegger soundboard, interrupting the class with phrases like, "Get to da choppa!"

One day, more bored than usual during a lecture on Excel, I decided to find out exactly how many cells were in an Excel document. I spent nearly ten minutes scrolling my cursor to the right and downward. In case you were wondering, it's just shy of a bajillion. When I finally arrived at the bottom of this vast digital landscape, as a pioneer might stake a flag on the top of an unclimbed mountain, I thought it wise to sign my name in the final cell. Satisfied with my conquest, I resumed paying attention when we were assigned a task.

Forty minutes later, the class was nearing the end and we were instructed to print the one-page document we'd been diligently crafting. Like everyone else, I complied.

The industrial classroom printer roared to life and began churning out completed assignments one by one. All was well as students lined up to collect their printed single-page documents. That is, until one young lady announced that completed assignments were no longer being printed, but rather sheet after sheet of empty cells instead.

The teacher shuffled over hastily to investigate. He diagnosed that the printer was, indeed, puking up countless sheets of wasted paper. He immediately employed the fix most people used for uncooperative technology back then: a couple of open-palmed smacks upside the thing, as if a swift dose of abuse might jostle loose whatever solution they were hoping for.

Perhaps it's my cloudy teenage memory, or even a writer's subconscious trick to embellish for humor, but when that failed, I'm pretty sure smoke began billowing into the ceiling as the machine worked on overdrive.

Somewhere after the hundredth page was spewed forth, that crotchety old fart snapped. "Who is printing all these sheets!?" he yelled. *"Who is printing all these sheets!?"* That's when I remembered signing my name in the depths of the Excel world.

"WHO IS PRINTING ALL THESE SHEETS!?" the teacher yelled once more.

"GET TO DA CHOPPA!" Arnold yelled back from somewhere in class.

As wildly entertaining as our teacher's reaction was for the whole class, I began sweating, knowing he'd find out exactly who was printing all those sheets after an entire rainforest had been chopped down.

By this time, our poor teacher was hunched over that conflabbit piece of technology, button mashing all the controls. "How do you stop this thing!?" he cried.

"If it bleeds, we can kill it!" Arnold replied.

"*How do you stop this thing!?*" he cried.

"I need your clothes, your boots, and your motorcycle!" Arnold replied.

"*HOW DO YOU STOP THIS THING!?*" he cried.

"Come with me if you want to live!" Arnold replied.

That's when I placed an assuring hand upon the teacher's shoulder and reached for the power cord. I yanked it from the socket and the excessive whine of tired printer wheels slowed to a halt and the imaginary smoke cleared. Our teacher exhaled a huge sigh of relief. Then he looked at me with a big smile and said, "Son, you're a hero."

But in the relieved silence of the classroom, another voice rang out: "I'll be back."

SOCIAL DEVIANCE

"Entering a conversation that you'd overheard
but hadn't been invited to join
was sort of like peeing in someone's coffee
while they stood there and watched you do it."
—*Johnny B. Truant*

What events lead up to a high school boy being strangled by a man twice his age and thrice his size, you ask? Well, let me tell you.

In the 11th grade, I took a Sociology class. One day, our former hippie turned crew-cut teacher brought up a topic called "Social Deviance." I had no idea what it was at the time, but as a young teenage boy, it certainly rolled off the tongue nicely. The teacher explained that social deviance is a behavioral violation of social norms. These could range from the extreme, such as murder, to the slight, such as jaywalking. He explained that this phenomenon exists in all societies where there are norms, and that in the face of these norms, there exist two possibilities: conform or defy. There were even deeper layers to consider, such as how some behaviors both conform and defy. He used the example of a speed limit for a class coming of age to get their license. Speeding is technically a legal violation, he told us, but also a conformity, as most of society drives above the limit.

At this point, the class was assigned a project. We were to partner up and observe as many of the more common social norms we could find. Then, we were to choose any one of them and gently—*gently*—push the boundaries. Outside of murder, we were pretty much left to our creative liberties. But whatever we chose, we had to capture video evidence of reactions and present them to the class in one month's time.

Looking back, I'm not so sure this was the best assignment for kids our age. While I can't speak for the girls, I will say that permission for teenage boys to break rules took naturally existing levels of social deviance and opened the floodgates. In our teacher's defense, though, he did offer one feeble piece of advice before he sent us off into the world. He said that although the word "deviance" may have a negative connotation, positive deviation from norms—such as being kind to strangers—also qualifies. This was promptly ignored.

I was on the younger end of the spectrum of kids in my grade, so I was yet to pass the driver's exam. Fortunately, my partner already had his license, because asking one of our parents to drop us off at an upscale outdoor mall dressed in full camouflage and war paint may have raised questions.

We chose The Promenade Shops in Evergreen Valley for two reasons: 1) It was located in our high school rival's neighboring town, and 2) It was an upscale environment where waltzing around like a combat veteran would surely qualify as deviant.

According to their website (and remember to extend your pinky as you read), "The Promenade Shops at Evergreen Valley offer an outstanding collection of the most coveted specialty retailers around." With a quaint and peaceful ambiance provided by a large fountain, tree-lined walkways, and fire pit seating, "Evergreen Valley is sure to please."

Sure to please indeed, I thought. *Please our class with some juicy reactions!*

My intention was to "hide" in plain sight against backdrops that made absolutely no sense. For example, I'd lie prone on a concrete walkway, "hidden" behind a small planter of flowers. Or I'd stand with my back against a brick wall, arms asplay, along a building on the main sidewalk. My partner was to capture the befuddled stares of shoppers as I pretended they couldn't see me. Sometimes, for the more curiously involved onlookers, I'd raise a finger to my lips and, *Shhhh,* in the manner in which Elmer Fudd might hunt wabbits.

My fantasy of lighthearted amusement and humorous reactions was cut short as a golf cart zoomed up the sidewalk out of nowhere and screeched to a halt before me. A man speaking into a walkie-talkie dismounted and swiftly approached as he announced, "Copy that. I found him." In bold black lettering on his bright yellow shirt read the word **SECURITY**.

He towered over me as he fired off heated questions. He was far from amused by my little charade. He hammered me with an inquisition about who I was, what I was doing, and why I was dressed that way.

At first, the excuse of, "My teacher made me do it!" fell on deaf ears. He wasn't in the mood for games and didn't find that answer very appealing. Then, my classmate emerged from across the street holding a camera and helped defuse the situation. The man calmed down but asked us to accompany him to the security office anyway. We didn't even realize this place had security, let alone a security *office*.

He led us into a room with monitors displaying various camera angles of the grounds, surveillance being something else we failed to see. He sat us down at a desk and gave us a thorough interrogation. We explained the best we could the nature of our project—about needing to capture reactions, about how we were just a couple of bookworms trying to get a good grade, about why this may be our only chance to earn a scholarship to university. After we'd had our turn, he shared the kinds of reactions we'd actually inspired: ones of fear, ones of anxiety, ones of reporting a militiaman snooping around the property.

Mission accomplished, I thought. *Social Deviance at its finest!*

I did my best to hide the joy that this story would surely earn us an A. I appeared stoic, acting as though I understood the severity of our actions. After nodding in agreement that we'd done an inconsiderate thing, he told us to erase all the footage we'd taken. I tried to plead that our grade depended on that film and a smirk flashed across his face. Instead of sympathizing, he told us that we were lucky he didn't have us arrested. In hindsight, I'm not sure how much jail time a minor would have served for the heinous crime of, well, being a teenager, but life in prison seems unlikely. At the time, though, his threat was enough to scare us into complying.

Because Social Deviance project A was confiscated, my classmate and I had no other choice but to come up with Social Deviance project B. The next day, we took our camera to a local grocery store to mess with shoppers. We began with stunts like placing items from their carts into our own as we strolled on by. In some cases, we'd even stolen carts altogether when someone wasn't looking, just as it appeared they were shopping for their last item. The deviance escalated when I wandered down an aisle where a lone woman was standing, peering into the shelves. I took my post across from her and pretended to do the same.

On film later, we'd watch as I turned, tapped her on the shoulder, then quickly snapped around to pretend I was reading a label. When the woman turned to find me staring at a jar, she scanned up and down the aisle to look for other suspects. When she saw no one, her face scrunched in confusion, but eventually she resumed her task. I once more repeated the same, and we'd watch her turn, frown, and stare me down for a good long while. But then, as if nothing ever happened, I'd place the jar in my basket and walk away.

After we'd collected enough deviance on film, my partner and I were standing at the front of the store, patting ourselves on the back for a job well done. That's when the woman I'd tapped on the shoulder appeared from the aisle next to us and said, "*There* he is!"

A stocky man with a mean mug and sour face appeared beside her. He took one look at me and got right up in my face. He pointed his finger a pimple's distance away from my nose and growled, "Were *you* the one touching *my* wife?"

Fear flooded me. I began to meekly explain that it was just a humorous gag for a school project, but the very sound of my voice infuriated him.

Looking back, he didn't appear to be the type who'd once tossed his cap into the air at graduation to cheer, "We did it!" No, a compassionate understanding for "school" "projects" was never within this man's emotional repertoire. He was more likely the dropout bully that snacked on dweebs like me, knocking out more teeth than he'd earned A's or B's. Picturing him now, I would have done better to point behind him and shout, "*That's* the guy you're looking for over there!" Then promptly run away.

"You think this is *funny*!?" he asked, loud enough to capture the stares of everyone around us. And to be fair, when he put it like that, the whole project—social deviance in general, really—no longer inspired warm and giddy feelings. It inspired more of that gut-clenching feeling when you suspect your life is in danger.

His eyes blazed with rage as he stepped even closer to repeat himself, his foul breath violating my nose. "I asked if you think this is *funny*!?"

I've always had a knack for recognizing the irrational glimmer in a crazy man's eye, but what happened next surprised even me.

As I began to stammer an explanation—how this was all a big misunderstanding, how I'd love to offer an apology, how I promised never to do anything so criminal as tap another woman on the shoulder again—he lunged forward and wrung his hands around my neck, tackling me into the display of cans behind me. Beans clattered to the floor as I was pinned to the ground with this man on top of me. He pressed his full weight into my throat as the rings of my trachea were compressed and my life squeezed away. Stars appeared, and although the scene began to go dark, I distinctly remember seeing the devil in his eyes as he screamed, "I've been to prison, and I ain't afraid to go back!"

Here, I peed. Not by choice, as one doesn't often choose to pee oneself in public, but out of a natural reaction in the face of a life-threatening nightmare. You see, in summoning the "fight-or-flight" response, the body will discharge any unnecessary weight that could slow it down in the event of a getaway. In this case, though, there was no getaway. I was just pinned to the toppled display of cans by my neck, peeing.

In addition to my own urination, I was enlightened to this man's urinary habits when he told me, "If you *ever* touch my wife again, I will rip your head off and piss down your throat!"

I suppose a thinking man could have grabbed a can of beans and driven it into this man's temple, but my oxygen-deprived brain was simply focused on wheezing any air it could breathe. I failed to think so clearly and instead just blacked out. Momentarily at least, because the next thing I remember, my friend and I were sprinting for the car.

Now, when it came time to turn in our Sociology project, it turned out we were the only ones who even dared to attempt filming social deviance. But instead of rewarding us with an A and giving everyone else F's like any rational human being would do, our teacher simply scrapped the project altogether. So in the end, it turned out I was strangled by a stranger for absolutely no reason.

OMELET TRAIN

"You cannot make an omelet
without breaking some balls."
—*Margaret Thatcher*

Before I took my first step into the real world as a line cook at the age of sixteen, I had the idea that all adults had their shit together. Being dropped into a restaurant surrounded by degenerates burst that bubble of ignorance faster than an egg being tossed off a three-story building.

I had a fairly strict upbringing, you see, which shielded my knowledge of life outside our small town, limited neighborhood friends, and a few well-managed extracurricular activities. I imagined the world was a rather wholesome place before being employed at the local branch of a diner chain. My hiring manager, Carlos, had graduated from my high school a few years before me. He recognized my innocence and decided to take me under his wing, assigning me to the breakfast crew so we could work the same hours. That crew included two other cooks, Booker and John.

Booker was an impressively muscular dark-skinned fellow in his forties. It was rumored that he could bench press over four-hundred pounds back in the day—"back in the day" referring to his years spent in prison for grand theft auto. Now, Booker was making up for lost time by spending every weekend in the club, boozing and more than just dabbling with cocaine. Because of this, he could often be found standing in front of the grill with a spatula in hand, fast asleep. His unconscious teetering threatened a face-plant into the burning eggs that were supposed to be served over-easy.

John had also graduated from my high school, though decades earlier. When I met him, he was balding with a big gut from drinking away the stress of both a secondary job to pay child support and the hatred of his ex-wife. He wore thick spectacles that magnified the fact that only one eye saw straight while the other veered rogue. His personality was abrasive at best, and his demeanor inspired what a less sympathetic person might call "white trash."

Despite all of this, John loved to relive his glory days by telling stories of when he was a football star. He claimed to have fucked a hundred girls by the time he graduated high school. This blew my mind for three reasons. 1) I couldn't imagine any girl would let this man inside of her, 2) I didn't even *know* a hundred girls, and 3) I was still a virgin at the time. When John caught wind of this last one, he stared at me in disbelief.

"What are you, *gay* or something?" he said in a patronizing tone.

"What!? No!" I struggled for words. "I, well, I- I- I don't know. The opportunity just hasn't come up yet, I suppose." The truth was I was just awkward and shy.

"He plays *soccer*," yelled Carlos from across the restaurant, slandering the sport as if it was a disgrace.

"*Pfft!*" John laughed from deep within his belly. "That sport's for fags!" This was news to me, but Carlos and Booker must have agreed as they enjoyed a healthy laugh as well.

Former high school quarterback turned funny-guy waiter, Derek, popped his head into the food window and chimed in, "Did I hear something about soccer playin' faggots!?" Then they all burst out laughing again. As Derek punched a food order into the computer, he said, "Got somethin' for you boys!" Then he winked at me and snapped his fingers into a this-one's-for-you-pal kind of gun as he walked away.

As the ticket was churned out in the kitchen John ripped it off the printer for inspection. "Uh oh, Booker," he said gravely. He shook his head and added, "This doesn't look good."

"Why, what is it, John?" Booker played along. John showed Booker the ticket, which Booker examined carefully. He also shook his head gravely, and with regret, he agreed, "No. No, that doesn't look good *at all*."

John cocked his head back like a wolf at the moon and cried out for the whole restaurant to hear, "Chooooo-chooooo!"

Booker slapped John's back as he keeled over in laughter. Derek popped his head back in the food window and reached in the air to grasp an invisible pull-string. With a couple of playful tugs he blew a train-whistle of his own. "Chooooo-chooooo!"

John chugged the ticket along some invisible tracks in the air as he began chanting, "Chug-a chug-a chug-a chug-a...

Chug-a chug-a chug-a chug-a...

CHUG-a chug-a chug-a chug-a…"

"Chooooo-chooooo!" Carlos bellowed out from an unseen location before barging into the room. "Do I hear the train-a-comin'!?" he yelled, cupping a hand over his ear.

"Riiight on schedule!" Booker yelled. Then all four burst into another fit of laughter as the ticket was placed gingerly before me. They all waltzed out of the kitchen bouncing jokes around about soccer playin' fags and dispersing to flirt with waitresses and gawk at female customers.

Is this real life? I thought. *Jailbirds and train conductors?*

Upon the ticket were four omelets, and in our world, making omelets was considered the bottom of the totem pole. Nothing against omelets or consumers of omelets, but the recipe for omelets was a hassle, and they flowed in with such omelet-like abundance that you'd inevitably be overwhelmed with an onslaught of omelets during a Sunday morning rush of omelets.

Are you getting tired of the word "omelets"? Welcome to my omelety adolescence.

A carton of eggs—and I don't mean what you're envisioning now, I mean the cardboard rectangle a half gallon of milk comes in—was poured into a plastic plate until full. You had to lift the dripping plate into a microwave on a shelf about eye level, inevitably spilling some of the gooey liquid onto your chest and arms. Here, it was nuked to a semi-solid state before being removed again, and all the ingredients were added to the middle. The egg saucer was then folded on itself, a mound of cheese dumped on top, and microwaved for another thirty seconds to perfection.

If you weren't careful in removing it this time, making sure to keep the plate *perfectly* level, the whole thing would slip off the plate and tumble down your apron, legs, and shoes— something I learned on my own since no one had the courtesy to warn me. If that was the case, you had to start the process over, cleaning cheese out of your shoelaces as the microwave zapped your second attempt to completion. This time, with more caution, the omelet was slid onto a real plate with home-fries and placed into the food window for delivery. One down, four to go, ticket number one of the morning.

This train-wreck was a typical Sunday for me in those days. Occasionally, though, if I was lucky, I'd skirt the homosexual accusations for playing the world's greatest sport when their hangovers were severe. Booker could be found sitting comatose on a grease bucket behind the freezer, while John would bless me with his lethargic presence until his head could no longer stand the pounding. In the peak of the morning rush, he'd graciously announce, "Welp! I've had about enough of this." Then he'd remove his apron and clock out. There I would find myself—at sixteen, mind you—solely responsible for feeding an influx of customers at a reputable diner.

While swamped with tickets and drowning in omelets, Carlos would often come to the rescue offering encouragement like, "What the fuck is the holdup back here!?" He'd throw a pickle at Booker and yell, "Wake up!" Then he'd glare at me as if it was my fault an ex-convict who resembled Carl Weathers after a coke bender was snoozing on the job.

Startled, Booker would blink to consciousness and catch a glimpse of the clock. "Is that the time?" he'd say, slowly rising for a stretch. "Welp, I need to get goin'." And with a pat on my back, he'd say, "You got this," and leave.

While single-handedly operating two grills, a frialator, a microwave, and prepping plates of food, the ticket machine would continue churning out new orders endlessly. It was at this point that Derek would stick his head through the food window with a grin. "Got one for you, bo—" He'd pause short and look around before asking where everyone was. When I told him they'd left, he'd helpfully snap his fingers with a wink and say "Choo-choo, motherfucker!" as another long order of omelets rang through as the caboose of the train.

This first step into the "real world" shattered the barrier of a small, middle-class, suburban upbringing I was held behind in the days before a driver's license. Once I had the expense of a car, though, I needed a job, and the people I met at that job shaped much of my formative years. Carlos, as any responsible manager does, took me under his wing in other realms, too: mainly drinking. At one point, all of my sheltered and childhood best friends—Ken, Michael, and Jonathan—worked at the diner for Carlos. And he took it upon himself to show us the ways of booze.

The first time Carlos invited us over to his house to drink, we had to let him down, saying our parents weren't apt to let us stay out late. "There's a workaround for that," he told us: day drinking. Well, *morning* drinking, to be exact. That way we could sober up by the time we had to face our parents later that day.

The first time I was introduced to beer pong was at 9am. The rest of that memory, as you can imagine, is extremely fuzzy. But it clears up around the ride home, with the lingering sting of vomit in my throat and a woozy conversation with my mother about what we'd been up to. Ultimately, the lies were believed, and we got away with it. That experience set the tone for much of my adolescence to come.

Years later, a sober Carlos would reach out and tell me that John passed away at the age of only fifty-two. A gut feeling tells me the heavy drinking may have played a role, but that's way down the road. For now, we were all hoping on the booze train bright and early.

Choo-choo, motherfucker.

CARL

"I hate to advocate drugs, alcohol,
violence, or insanit to anyone,
but they've always worked for me."
—Hunter S. Thompson

It seemed like we were always speeding in our late teens, mostly because Carl was always driving. Carl was wildly impulsive—the type to get his nipples pierced on a whim, the type to take ecstasy for kicks on a casual evening—and he was always jazzed up on nicotine, booze, coke, adderall, or whatever he could get his hands on. Somewhere along the line, he adopted this "I'm-gonna-die-before-thirty-five-anyway" attitude, which, by association, we were all strapped into.

One time we arrived at a gas station, and Carl shut off the car alongside a pump. He got out and plugged a cigarette in his mouth, lighting it before he walked around to the other side to fill up on gas. Michael passed the bong back to Jack to be tucked under the seat as everyone piled out and disappeared inside the gas station. I chose to lay back and close my eyes.

After a brief and quiet moment of nursing the pounding in my skull, an increasingly louder *vrooooom* of a motorcycle fast approached. It was followed by the sudden *skirrrrt* of screeching brakes right outside my door. Before I could open my eyes to see what was going on, a leathered arm plunged through my open window and slapped me on the chest.

"Steveee!" yelled Carl excitedly.

"What the fuck, man," I said to the dismounting rider. "You almost gave me a heart attack."

"What's up, fellas?" said Steve, lifting his helmet and walking around the car to give Carl a hug. "You wanted a thirty, right?" Carl nodded, and Steve disappeared inside.

When Carl finished pumping gas, he hopped back in the car and popped the trunk. Steve returned shortly after, carrying a case of beer and laughing in the company of our other friends. He tossed the beer in the open trunk and slammed it shut. "Follow me," he said, mounting his bike once more.

We fired up the engines, and Steve rolled out of the gas station with Carl close behind. As we pulled out and filed into a line of cars at a red light, Jack discreetly took another rip from the bong and held it in his lungs. When the light turned green, Steve shot ahead, weaving through spaces only a bike could squeeze. Jack coughed up a big cloud that swirled right into Carl's eyes and yelled, "You're losin' him!"

Carl whipped his head around to glare at Jack. "I know that, you fucking degenerate!"

An absurd response could always be provoked from Carl with the right quip or banter, and we always found this amusing.

Carl turned around and flicked his cigarette out the window as Steve veered down a side road. Carl blared the horn at a creeping old lady as he yanked the car onto the shoulder to pass. He sped up to the side road, cranked the wheel around the turn, then floored it in the direction of the shrinking motorcycle. We zoomed down the road past a sign that read "SPEED BUMPS AHEAD."

As we flew down the quiet back road, Jack called out, "Yo, watch out for th—"

Ba-Dunk!

The car hit the speed bump going fifty as the passengers and all its contents were launched into the air. "I can't even see him anymore," yelled Jack, smoke from another rip billowing from his lips into the wind. "Drive faste—"

Ba-Dunk!

"Would you shut your *fuckin'* mouth," Ken laughed, rubbing the top of his head. Jack laughed along as Carl pressed the gas pedal even harder.

Ba-Dunk! Ba-Dunk! Ba-Dunk!

The suspension cried for mercy under the weight of six plus a thumping case of beer in the trunk. The drive opened up to a smooth stretch of country road when Carl took the car around a hard bend. As Jack was mushed into the door by the weight of Ken and me, the bong was knocked from his hands and spilled onto the floor. The putrid smell of swampy resin water pierced the wind and violated the air. As Carl bent the car around another curve, mushing me on the other side this time, he whipped his head around and screamed, "What the fuck is that smell!?"

"Watch the road!" yelled Ken.

Carl snapped his head back toward the road as we shot up and over a small hill. As we plunged downward, we saw Steve parked a short distance away at an intersection. Carl slammed on the brakes, and we screeched to a halt mere inches from the back of Steve's bike. A cloud of burnt rubber blew past us as we all exchanged expressions of relief.

"What the *FUCK*," Carl exploded as he whipped back around, "is that smell!?"

Jack ignored this for the second time as he shot forth a commanding finger an inch from Carl's nose. "Go!" he yelled as Steve's engine sailed down the road.

Carl whipped forward and yelled back, "You fucking *barn animals!*" The rest of us snickered as he stomped the accelerator. We blew through the stop sign as we flew down a narrow straightaway to close the gap behind Steve. The motorcycle took a sudden right turn into a driveway, and Carl went shooting right past him. He slammed on the brakes, and we screeched to a halt. Then he jammed the car in reverse and floored it backward. We passed the driveway a second time as he hit the brakes and jerked us to a stop again. Then he jammed the car into drive once more and cranked us into a driveway barely long enough to squeeze the vehicle off the road. He jammed the gear into park, ripped the key out of the ignition, shouldered open his door, and lurched out as he slammed it shut. "You're all *worthless!*" he screamed as he stormed up the walkway after Steve.

"Hey," said Michael, smiling as he turned to look for the bong. "Is there any more of that?"

"Fresh out," said Jack, opening his door to stand up for a casual stretch.

The rest of us clambered out of the car and made our way down the walkway. Steve was standing in the living room smiling with his hands on his hips and head tilted sideways. "What took you guys so long?" he asked.

"Our *driver* took his sweet time," said Jack as he walked by Carl, slapping him on the shoulder.

"These *ingrates* spilled their *bong* all over my fuckin' car," said Carl.

"Gross," laughed Steve as he offered an open palm toward the cellar door. "Meet me downstairs." Then he walked down the hallway toward his bedroom with Carl in tow.

Jonathan sauntered over toward the door and flipped the switch. The rest of us filed behind as he lumbered down a creaky set of stairs. We could barely make out a half-circle of couches beneath the one dimly lit ceiling bulb as we reached the bottom and peered around.

"He's gonna kill us with that driving," Ken said to me with a shaking head. "You know that, don't you?"

"Please," I said with a furrowed brow. "He's yet to kill us once!"

It wasn't long before Steve and Carl made their way downstairs. "You guys prefer it all dark like this?" said Steve, disappearing into the shadows of the far corner of the room. *Click.* The cellar became illuminated by a long blacklight over a pool table that was hidden in the dark. Jack and I exchanged a quick glance before hopping up to grab the cues off the table. Steve walked over and reached into his pocket to pull out a tiny bag. He popped it open and dumped a glowing white powder onto the rail. He began chopping it up with a credit card and said, "You guys down?"

There was a silent hesitation before Carl swaggered over to the rail and said, "*I'm* no pussy."

"Alriiight," said Steve.

Jack set me up for the break as Steve set Carl up for the blow. I took aim down the table as Carl took aim down his line and— *sniff! clack! bang!*—we were off. Steve pulled two joints from another pocket. He lit one and passed it to Jack then lit the other and passed it to me. "If you want beer it's there," said Steve, pointing to a fridge behind the couches. Michael didn't hesitate for a second before he walked over and yanked it open. He filled his arm with bottles before he made his way around the room.

Carl looked at me rubbing a sniffling nose and said, "Steve showed me his safe." Then he paused to stare deep into my eyes and made sure I was paying attention. "There was a *pound* of weed in there."

"Dayyyum!"

"Guns, coke, molly," said Carl, leaning on my shoulder, cracking up with laughter. "I love Steve!" Then he suddenly became serious, pulling a large bag of marijuana from his pocket. "Here," he told me as he slapped the bag into my hand. "Four hundred. Twenty for the beer."

"Sweet!" I said, turning to Jack to show him. Jack was standing with the joint between his lips and his beer cap to the edge of the pool table, palm raised high in the air. "Jack, they're"—S*lam!* He whacked the top of the bottle, and the cap went rattling to the floor—"twist offs…"

"Oops," said Jack as he turned to see Steve staring at his pool table, frozen in disbelief.

There was a long and awkward pause before Steve bent over and blew a line of coke. Then he put his own bottle to the table and slammed his palm. The cap went rattling to the floor as he pushed his beer toward Jack and said, "Didn't know that little trick!" They cheers-ed and each took a swig laughing.

"Quit fuckin' up his table and pay the man," I told Jack, tossing him the bag of weed.

Jack caught it with a smile and said, "That's what I like to see!" Then he reached into his pocket for a wad of cash and handed it to Steve.

We played until the last ball was sunk before we told Steve it was time to hit the road. We wanted to make it to the beach before the morning crowd shuffled in.

When we got to the car, I grabbed the bong and handed it to Jack. "Put this in the trunk with the weed already, would ya?"

He took it smiling with beat-red eyes and yelled, "Carl! Trunk!" Carl finished lighting a cigarette and popped the trunk as he fired up the engine. The rest of us piled into the car. Jack slammed the trunk closed and walked back around carrying two cans of beer.

"Seriously?" I asked as he climbed in and shut the door.

"Road sodas," he replied. Jonathan heard and reached back over his shoulder with an open palm without even turning around. Jack slapped a can in his hand and the beer disappeared into the front seat.

As we retraced our path down the same winding roads, Jack lifted his beer and pulled the tab. *Crack!*—the can exploded spraying everyone inside. "What the fuck was that!?" screamed Carl, snapping his head around to find Jack slurping up the volcano of froth erupting onto his seat.

"Watch the road!" yelled Ken.

"Where the fuck's mine?" asked Carl, shifting his gaze to the road again. *Crack!*— Jonathan exploded the front seat can all over the windshield and passed an erupting volcano toward Carl. "What the fuck's wrong with you!?" yelled Carl as his lap filled with foam. Jonathan withdrew the can and slurped the foam himself. Carl smeared the beery splatter with an old fast-food bag in a failed attempt to wipe the windshield clean.

"Here," said Jack, leaning forward to tilt his can toward Carl's mouth. Carl pursed his lips while he glanced back-and-forth from road to can.

Just as Jack began pouring him a sip—*Ba-Dunk!*—a splash of beer speed-bumped into Carl's lap. "You fucking *Jew*!" he screamed.

Ken eyed Jack as Jack withdrew the can. Jack shrugged unfazed and said, "It's accurate," taking a casual sip of his own.

"Well, that was rude," said Michael, first looking at Carl, then turning toward Jack, "not to grab enough for the rest of us!"

Carl pushed the pedal to the floor as we *Ba-Dunk! Ba-Dunk! Ba-Dunk!*-ed back to the main road. Ken dumped his face in his hands and shook his head as the car swung onto the main drag and zoomed toward the highway.

Michael finished the rest of the front seat beer and tossed the can over his shoulder at my feet. I drank what was left of the one we had in the back and then kicked both empties into a McDonald's bag under the seat in front of me.

A great song came on the radio as we approached a long straightaway up a gradual hill and Carl cranked the volume. He stomped the accelerator, mashed down all the window buttons, and amidst a storm of air guitaring, beat tapping, and lyric screaming, we shot over the crest of the hill, nearly airborne. We bounced back on the road at the same time we all caught a glimpse of our worst nightmare: a state trooper, tucked on the shoulder, radar gun pointed right at us.

The radio blared on for a moment longer before Carl jumped on the brakes. He fumbled onto the OFF switch, but it was too late. We all watched in the rearview mirror as the flashing red-and-blue pulled onto the road and came screeching down the hill after us.

Carl rolled the car onto a dusty shoulder, parked it, and turned off the engine. The cruiser pulled up close behind, kicking up a cloud of dust all around. An eternity passed as the flashing lights reflected brightly in the rearview mirror and the car grew warmer in the blazing sun. The tension in a car full of clenched hearts grew thick and dreary as more time slipped by. Empty beer cans and a failed breathalyzer would be one thing for an underaged driver, but the addition of a bong, thirty-rack, and ounce of weed in the trunk could be a defining moment in a young man's life.

The dust had long settled by the time the trooper finally emerged from his vehicle. My heart sank even lower as he sauntered toward our car. He hiked up his gun belt with a twist as he arrived at the driver's-side door and casually leaned onto our window with one arm and pressed the other into his nightstick as he bent over to get a good look around. The trooper said nothing as he stared through his dark glasses at the grave expressions that avoided his gaze. He built even more suspense as he slowly twitched his mustache side to side as he thought what to say. Finally, with a deep, intimidating voice he broke the silence.

"Why are there three of you in the front?" he asked.

Carl turned to the man and meekly explained how his car was actually designed this way, that everyone was clicked safely into seat belts. The trooper wore a stone expression and continued to stare back in silence. After a few more twitches of the 'stache, he slowly nodded his head. It seemed he'd bought into Carl's bumbling on the matter, but then he asked the real question in an even sterner tone.

"Do you have any idea how fast you were going?"

Carl cleared his throat in nervous acknowledgement before he squeaked. "*Too* fast..?"

"License and registration," said the policeman.

Carl fumbled through his glovebox to unbury his registration and handed it over along with his ID. We reassumed our suspenseful silence as the trooper walked back to his vehicle.

"This is bullshit," whispered Carl. "The only reason he pulled us over is because we have three up front." He mumbled on about his innocence, claiming he was only driving the speed of traffic as a timeless spell went by. Eventually the officer opened his cruiser door once again. He approached again, bent over, and handed Carl his license and registration. Then he handed him a speeding ticket and said some parting words before returning to his own car. As the cruiser pulled off the shoulder and roared on down the road, there was a collective sigh of relief when it was safely out of view. It was a ticket, but, considering the circumstance, *only* a ticket.

Ken broke the silence by saying, "We just got *so* luck—"

"THIS! IS! *BULLSHIT!*" Carl raged. He jammed his registration and ticket back into the glovebox, then he fetched a cigarette and plugged it in his mouth with a light. He cranked the key to start the engine and said, "I'm fighting this," as he slapped the radio back on. Then he ripped the gear into drive and punched the gas pedal. The tires spun out in the dirt for a moment before the car shot off the shoulder, and a cloud of dust lingered behind as we sped down the road even faster than before.

THE REBUBLICAN

*"There may be a great fire in our soul,
yet no one ever comes to warm himself at it,
and the passers-by see only a wisp of smoke."*
—*Vincent van Gogh*

I smoked a lot of weed as a young man, the reasons and methods for doing so were numerous. Experimentation, my crowd, and psychological motives were some of the former, but here I'd like to focus on the latter.

A bowl, I would say, was the go-to method for my friends and me. I couldn't even venture a guess as to how many bowls I've smoked in the company of old friends, new friends, strangers, or solitude. Joints, of course, were also popular, sometimes spliffed with a bit of tobacco from a cigarette for that little extra boost. One summer, my friends and I even rolled a few cross-joints after we saw the movie *Pineapple Express*. Emptying the guts of a cigar and stuffing it with weed to make a blunt was another frequent method. And if we were feeling ambitious, sometimes we'd empty the contents of a wood-tipped Black & Mild and fill the whole thing with weed as well. There were bongs and gravity bongs and other homemade contraptions—sometimes using a water bottle or even a seashell—but my favorite method, and the one I'd like to discuss here, was a red, white, and blue bubbler in the shape of a seated elephant. You packed the weed on the top of his head and smoked through the pipe of his trunk. Because of his patriotic colors, and perhaps the freedom he stood for, we dubbed him "The Rebublican."

The Rebublican served us loyally for a good couple of years before he met an early demise (or assassination as one conspiracy rumor floats amongst our circle of friends). We did our best to fill him with the finest black market weeds money could buy. You see, in the days before decriminalization, the means of getting your hands on some good marijuana weren't always easy. My friends and I were often dealing with characters that resembled Sideshow Bob from *The Simpsons* or venturing into some sketchy neighborhood just to get high.

There was the time Carl and I drove into the depths of some ghetto, as per the referral of a "friend" of his. We coughed up four-hundred bucks to some hoodlum who met us on a street corner. "Wait here," the guy told us after counting the wad of cash. Then he disappeared into an apartment building before we could even mention we'd prefer to tag along. We were parked along the curb for twenty minutes like sitting ducks as the local riffraff strolled by eyeing our preppy clothes. Carl had his arm out the window holding a cigarette, in the middle of asking if I thought we'd been robbed, when a mysterious hooded figure appeared from nowhere, shoved his hand through the open window, and then as quickly as he'd come, was gone again. An ounce of weed had appeared in Carl's lap in that split second of time.

Our buddy Ken once connected us with an ex-military acquaintance of his. The guy informed Ken that he had access to medical-grade marijuana from California, air-sealed and shipped right to his doorstep. He agreed to meet with Jack and me to hook us up with a deal.

At dusk, a sleek, black Infinity four-door with limousine tints on all sides pulled up to our driveway. The rear door popped open and a wave of hip-hop and a cloud of smoke poured outside. We climbed into the back seat and no greetings or eye contact were exchanged. A man who resembled Wesley Snipes in both demeanor and stature simply passed us the blunt he was smoking. "I gotta pick up my boy real quick," he yelled over the music. And with that, we zoomed off into the night.

Jay-Z's album *The Blueprint 3* was cranked even louder as we hit the entrance ramp of the highway. The blunt circled the car numerous times as we blasted off into a medical-grade high. Words were never spoken; there was no point. The bass of the speakers would have swallowed them whole. We smoked the blunt down to the roach as we sped along for the entire duration of the album. At one point, I felt too high to even be a passenger, never mind wrap my head around how this guy was still *driving*. When the first song began to repeat itself, Jack and I exchanged concerned looks that said, "Where the fuck is this ex-military drug dealer taking us?"

The answer eluded us until halfway through the second loop of the album, when we finally arrived outside a sketchy apartment building somewhere in the middle of nowhere. We parked and waited. No one said anything. After a few minutes, a tall silhouette appeared outside the tinted windows. It opened the passenger door, and a similar-looking man entered the car. He pounded fists with our driver and then appeared caught off guard when he saw a couple of squinting figures with ghostly complexions in the back seat. He stared back and forth between us skeptically before revealing a blunt of his own, already ablaze. He offered it toward us, and despite being high as the moon, Jack accepted the offer with a nod. Then we zoomed off into the darkness as the second and third loop of the same album spun to completion.

The time Jack had a gun pointed in his face, or when he was roped into a sting operation by policemen who'd caught him smoking on campus, are tales for another time. The point is, we did what we had to do as countrymen who honored The Rebublican. And this sometimes involved performing what we called "strikeouts."

"Now here's what you're gonna do," Michael told me one weekend. He sat me down at our party-provision-filled table and swept his arm across an already wet and sticky surface, knocking half-drunk cups of who-knows-what onto the floor. He slid over the nearest emptied shot glass and filled it with whatever was left in the closest bottle. Then he slammed a cold beer on the table so hard that it knocked one of the legs loose.

"First," he said, "you're gonna take a hit from that bubbler. *Before* you exhale," he went on, grabbing the shot glass and quivering it in front of my face like a bell, "take this shot. *Then,*" he said, opening the exploding can of beer, "chug that. When you finish, you can breathe again."

Too drunk to think twice, I followed his steps without hesitation: hit, shot, chug. All the while I was chugging, Michael, Jack, and Carl were chanting, "Striiike-out! Striiike-out! Striiike-out!" When I finally slammed the empty beer can down on the table, tears in my eyes and coughing up a hopsy cloud, Michael smacked me on the back and said, "Atta-boy!"

That's the last thing I remember of the night, but the next morning when we gathered in the kitchen to nurse our hangovers, we found a pile of red, white, and blue glass on the kitchen floor. There was an awkward pause and a jaw-dropping look of horror upon Carl's face before he ended the silence with jittery anger. "Who—the *fuck!*—broke The Rebublican!?"

Bethany, Jonathan's younger sister, eventually fessed up.

A year or so later, I drove to Jonathan's family home to pay them a visit. I parked my car in the street to find a cop standing in his front doorway. Alarmed, thinking someone was hurt, I began to run up to find out what happened. Another officer stepped out of the cruiser parked along the street and intercepted my path.

"Where do you think you're going, pal?"

"What's going on?" I asked.

"Never mind that," said the officer, staring into my eyes and looking for… something. "Let's take a look inside your car."

"Excuse me?" I shot back. "For what?"

"I think you know what," said the officer, stepping into my personal space now.

I stared at him and said, "I have no idea what you're talking about…"

He must have sensed I was telling the truth because his demeanor changed. "How do you know Bethany?" he asked more calmly, still looking back and forth between my eyes.

"She's my friend's sister. We grew up together. What's going on?"

"We're conducting a search for heroin."

"*What!?*"

Hearing the word "heroin" hit me like a bowling ball. He might as well have told me this Christian, church-going family had been smuggling tigers into the country or something equally absurd. I had, of course, heard of heroin, but as something that existed in faraway news reports, or ghettos, or the 1960s. Never would I have expected to find out that my boring hometown was

a hotspot in a heroin *epidemic*, let alone that someone I knew—
or at least thought I knew—like a little sister would be the target
of a search in a house I'd grown up in. This was a girl who had
shamed her brother and me for years about how much weed we
smoked. She'd spit out these fiery remarks about how smoking
was bad for you, how much it changed you and made you boring.
Meanwhile, she was chasing the dragon. To say I was caught off
guard would be an understatement. Part of my innocence and
naiveté was shattered that day—the part that hadn't realized
sometimes bad things can go on right under your nose.

After the police left, I found out that Bethany's boyfriend
had been pulled over shortly before they came knocking. He'd
ratted her out in an attempt to lessen his own punishment by the
law. Turns out he was the one who got her wrapped up in the
drug in the first place. About a year or so before, they had scored
some coke to celebrate his birthday. After they snorted the first
line, they realized it wasn't coke at all. Their dealer had pulled a
switcheroo and gave them heroin instead. *Boom*—both were
addicted instantly. They spent the next year struggling to quit,
finally reaching a point where they had each weaned down to
their last half-bag when he got pulled over and things blew up in
their face.

In a way, it could have been seen as a blessing—minus being
arrested, of course—because they were both sent to rehab
centers to try to turn their lives around. Unfortunately, Bethany
never got back on her feet again. She dropped out of school,
failed to maintain a steady job, and bounced from place to place
after her mother kicked her out when she relapsed again. The last
text Bethany sent to her brother was one celebrating thirty days
of sobriety. She was found dead of an overdose in the following
days.

I was at work when Jonathan called. I left the office immediately, barely able to hold myself together. On the drive home, I felt as though I was in some disillusioned reality, or maybe a bad dream. For a short time, I thought I was having a heart attack, the way my present existence seemed to slip from grasp.

Bethany was only the second person I'd lost that I was close to, the first being my grandmother who stuck around almost a year after the doctors told us she had only a few weeks to live. Her death was expected, even joked about. "You still suckin' up oxygen, Grandma?" she'd hear me say whenever she answered my calls. But Bethany's was sudden, out of the blue, and it ripped a hole in my perspective on how fragile life can be.

The atmosphere at my grandmother's funeral was full of sorrow, but it also carried the vibe of a celebration. She had lived a good, long life, and the love in the air from all her friends and relatives was palpable. Bethany's service was a mood of shock, even horror. The room was ice-cold in the tragic loss of a girl who'd perished before her time. Many who later wished they could have gotten up to speak remained frozen in their chairs.

In the weeks following Bethany's funeral, I got a tattoo in her honor. It's a pair of dice to represent how much our fate is a lucky roll, and they're melting, to remind me that whatever roll you get, it's only temporary.

I try to end most of my writings with a joke, or a twist, or a clever circle back around, but to do so here would only take away from honoring the memory of Bethany and the lessons her life has taught me. Instead, the end will come in the manner of which both she and The Rebublican met theirs: abrupt and broken.

SNOW

"Cocaine is a helluva drug."
—Dave Chapelle as Rick James

We all know that feeling of being hopped up on speed, wildly skiing through trees high on weed.

I started skiing when I was four years old and was pretty good by the time I got to college, where I met Ryan, who was also quite skilled. Over time, Ryan and I discovered another mutual interest: adderall. When combined, we found these two interests to be a powerful recipe for a good time.

When the weather called for snow, Ryan and I would make trips from UConn to Vermont. Sometimes we'd wake up at four in the morning, drive three hours north, ski all day, and still make it back in time to sleep before class the next day. This was no easy feat but one made doable with stimulation.

First, we'd hit the gas station for coffee, then fly down the night's empty roads, climbing into the mountains as the sun pierced over the horizon. The real fun began when the adderall kicked in as we puffed on joints during a hotbox of the very first gondola. By the time we reached the peak, with doors parting amidst a fog of smoke billowing away, we were as high as the clouds that floated around the summit. We'd do that awkward ski boot march toward the edge of the first run, step into our skis, and then—*fwoom!*—we were racing for the bottom.

This cycle was repeated until lunchtime. We'd pack sandwiches and snacks in our bags to avoid the crowded lodge. Eating hot soup amongst the roar of a cabin scene was nice, but skiing deep into the woods where the only sound was that of falling snow was more appealing.

By the time we'd exhausted ourselves on the slopes, we'd still have a considerable drive home. The adderall buzz is a long one, but I remember smoking American Spirits with the icy windows rolled down just to keep our eyes open as the tail end of the buzz faded away.

That thrill of skiing through glades high in the mountains, cruising up and down highways with my friend, and squeezing adventures into the short daylight hours of winter were some of the best times I've had. Of course, this was back when I loved to walk the tightrope of uppers and downers. A few years later, I'd sobered up, and returning to the slopes was never the same.

The question I have is: Did I ruin the experience for myself later on, or did I live it up while I was young?

The summer before that year at school, Ryan and I worked a university grounds maintenance job with a guy named Jerry. Jerry was a fifty-year-old bald man with his hat tipped back like Alvin the Chipmunk and the personality to match. There were other guys, too, of course. Three of us couldn't maintain the entire campus; we smoked way too much weed for that. Jerry and the rest of the full-time staff had help from ten other students our age, and that place attracted an assortment of characters.

There was Lapin, as we called a senior by his last name, who'd basically thrown away his accounting major to become a university landscaper. He was the type to lock himself in his mother's basement and play first-person shooter games for hours. He was a tad awkward at this whole life thing and seemed to find himself at home amongst the full-time misfits.

There was "Dumbass Dave," as his fraternity brothers called him. They'd often remind him, "You're so fucking dumb!" To which Dave would laugh as he stared off into the distance, puffing a Marlborough, nodding in agreement as if stupidity was a badge of honor. To be fair, he brought it upon himself. He lied during the interview process, for example, saying he had loads of experience with ride-on mowers. Then he drove one straight into a lake within an hour's time. Where Dave wasn't a dumbass, though, was in shipping pounds of weed from Oregon through vacuum-sealed bags. We'd often drive to his house over lunch to rip bongs before heading back to swing weed-whackers around.

But that was life at Landscape that summer: driving mowers into ponds and driving management insane, regretting their hire of so many potheads to maintain the beloved campus. But who better, really? We were both the worst group of bums you'd want operating gas-powered equipment with spinning blades, but also, in some curious way, the best men for the job.

I say this because there's a wonderful bond between the spacey virtues of getting high and the monotonous task of trimming grass. Landscaping a campus and smoking weed were made for each other. You could get lost in an endless sea of daydreams or transported into the world of music, all while slashing weeds around fence lines for hours at a time. It was the perfect job for hooligans like us.

Wood chippers, for example, were a thrilling adventure when blitzed on cloud nine. The sound of branches being slashed to shreds paired with the sight of scraps being spewed into the back of a trailer was wildly entertaining. Plus, we got to wear hard hats on those occasions, and the echoey transfusion of sound enhanced the experience even more.

And the types of people I met at this job did wonders to influence my malleable young mind. Take Diego, for example. I could tell he was an old hand in this line of work the moment I met him. His face and arms were darkened by years of sun. This became more apparent when he raised his cap to scratch his forehead, revealing a receding hairline covering skin as white as mine, despite being Puerto Rican. It was as though he'd been wearing that same hat for decades, the sun charring a distinct border around his skull. The muscles of his face were fixed into a furrowed brow from years of squinting into the daylight, and his bottom jaw jutted outward, giving him an expression of perpetual disgust.

For a man who got piss drunk every night, Diego had an impressive streak of never missing a day of work in thirty-five years. In fact, he never had so much as a sniffle. "Viruses don't stand a *chance* in that environment!" our boss would say, describing a bloodstream pickled by booze. But despite being an alcoholic, Diego was a workhorse who labored as many days at sixty-five as he did at my age.

Likewise, Diego never missed a day of fishing in all those years. Every morning when I arrived at work, his beat-up Chevy Astro van would already be parked at the shop—a vehicle that doubled as both a storage unit for fishing gear and a place to bang hookers down by the river. I would find him in the garage most mornings, fueling up on coffee and cigarettes to thwart off a hangover you could smell through his pores. I would try to make small talk to break the ice and get to know him.

"Hey, Diego, you catch anything last night?"

His usual reply, roughened by fifty years of smoking and delivered with fumes of moonshine, was a typical, "Ehhhh, just a fuckin' *buzz*."

On occasion, though, he'd have a success story for me.

"Hey, Diego, you catch anything last night?"

"Yeah, a few crabs."

"Oh yeah?" I'd say, a lover of seafood myself. "What kind?"

"Whatever kind them hookers got! *sss! sss! sss! sssss!*" He'd keel over in fits of laughter that whistled through his partially toothless smile, then lean onto a truck as the hysterics turned to coughing up a pre-cancerous lung.

This sort of reaction only came if you caught him in a good mood, though—and by good mood, I mean still drunk from the night before. (Or, if he were feeling particularly ambitious, after he'd slugged down a beer or two for breakfast that morning.) You couldn't judge him for it, though; construction is a tough lifestyle. And besides, it's not like he had to operate a bulldozer later that day. Oh wait, yes, he did.

Stories of cheap and toothless river whores were not uncommon amongst the workers. I'd hear tales of blowjobs that exceeded the talents of their wives, complete with gagging impersonations and details of retracting the foreskin of a hairy and uncircumcised shaft.

This was the sex education of my teenage years. Grotesque as it may have been, I had little experience at the time, so I was eager to absorb whatever I could—not unlike a contraceptive sponge, if you will.

One morning, a few of us were taking a coffee break in the utility van. From the back seat, I heard the sounds of a woman screaming in ecstasy. The sounds were projecting from the iPhone of a new guy, the half-brother of a long-time foreman who had just moved here from Puerto Rico. The "half" referred to their mother, who had subsequent relations with an African American gentleman. Because of this, he had notably darker skin that enveloped his rather muscular frame. And because he made the mistake of wrapping a camouflage bandana around his head the first day on the job, he was henceforth known among the Puerto Ricans as "Black Rambo." (The only reason I heard the origin of this story was because I made the mistake of wearing a white bandana on my first day and was henceforth known as "The Karate Kid.")

When I turned around to investigate the source of these orgasmic cries, Rambo must have noticed my expression of disbelief. In wide-eyed wonder at the abilities of his new smartphone, he looked at me and mustered up two of the only broken-English words he knew. "Dis *goood.*"

Judging by the sounds belted out by the young woman, there was no doubt about that. But I couldn't wrap my mind around his judgment of *this* being an appropriate time to watch pornography—sitting in a construction van at nine in the morning with a bunch of grubby dudes. When I turned back to the driver's seat to share my questions with Rambo's half-brother, he just stared ahead as if all was normal and said, "Sounds like a video I've seen called Atomic Onion Booty."

You can recognize pornos by sound!? I wondered, at which point it immediately became something for my teenage spirit to aspire to.

Drinking on the job wasn't uncommon. In fact, at one time, before my tenure, it was the norm. That is to say, until the boss went out to the trucks one morning to look for a tool and opened a compartment side door, only to have a wall of empty beer cans come crashing down upon him.

"That's *it!*" he yelled as the last few cans rattled to the floor. "You fuckin' drunks have got to cut this shit out!"

Apparently, that put a damper on the whole getting blasted at work thing. From then on, employees had to settle for a more discreet and responsible level of on-the-job drinking. Things slowed down to a mere trickle of booze—an IV drip of elixir to keep the shakes at bay.

By the time I got there, having a drink or two on the job was mostly limited to Friday afternoons. Or maybe a Wednesday at lunch, if the job was tough. Or a Monday, if the weather was nice.

It was soon into my first summer working at Landscape that we made a pit stop at a liquor store after work one day. Diego was driving the van, I was in the back seat, and Hector was in the front. Hector was a fellow Puerto Rican and long-time friend of Diego. Diego got Hector the job soon after Hector got out of prison for stabbing someone. Rumor had it that the stabbee had called Hector a name he didn't very much care for. So, in a drunken fit of rage, Hector plunged a knife into his belly. Likely the same knife that was clipped to his belt as I sat two feet away in the van.

As Diego parked outside the liquor store, Hector wrapped his arm around the driver's seat, flashing the image of a switchblade he'd prominently tattooed to his own arm while in prison. He turned to me and growled, "You want somethin'?"

Hector always growled. That was just his voice: a deep, raspy growl.

"Oh, I- I- I'm not old enough," I stammered.

"Didn't ask that," Hector snapped back.

He was intimidating, yet at the same time, you knew he had a good heart—the kind that was willing to buy an underaged teen a beer after a hard day's work. His demeanor often inspired the feelings associated with a lovable teddy bear, just one that wouldn't hesitate to rip your guts out if the situation called for it, much like a real bear. It was a strange dichotomy in the sense that on one hand, you wanted to hug him, but on the other, you wanted to stay at least an arm's length away. You know, just far enough to dodge a blade if he decided to take a swing at you.

I tried my best to get on Hector's good side, though. For example, I would help him to his feet when he struggled to upright himself after a lunchtime nap because of his enormous beer belly, much like a turtle who'd been flipped over on his shell.

"Get him a tall boy," said Diego, smoke rising from his lips as he puffed down to the filter.

After Hector left the van, I couldn't help but ask, "Did he really stab someone just for calling him a name?"

"Hector don' take shit from *nobody*," was the answer I received. Silence ensued.

Hector returned a short time later with a brown paper bag. He reached inside and pulled out a 22oz can of beer and handed it to me. It was ice-cold. He reached inside the bag once more and handed Diego a beer as well. *Pshhh!*—the can erupted as Diego popped it open and slurped down half its contents. Hector reached in and pulled out his own beer as he tossed the bag on the floor. *Pshhh!*—his own can sounded off before he slugged it down in the same manner.

They each let out an "*Ahhh,*" then both turned to stare at my unopened can with skeptical eyes. An awkward tension filled the van as their gaze rose to meet mine. *Pshhh!* I lifted the beer to my lips and began sipping. It *was* refreshing, that was for sure. I could see why they enjoyed it so immensely.

We drank the beers in the parking lot while Hector told me about the time he got arrested for stealing a street sweeper. When the police pulled him over, they discovered three things: 1) Hector was not a city worker licensed to operate a street sweeper, 2) Hector didn't possess any kind of driver's license whatsoever, and 3) Hector was as drunk as any pedestrian might need to be to in order to steal a street sweeper without any kind of license whatsoever. When Hector tried to rationalize his behavior, explaining that he merely needed to borrow it for a quick drive down the block to buy cigarettes, for some reason the officer wasn't seeing the situation eye-to-eye. Apparently the officer was—How did Hector put it again? Oh yes—"unreasonable," so Hector spent the night in jail.

I had quite a nice buzz going by the time I finished my beer and was giddy with laughter by the time Hector finished telling his story. Hector then took the empties and stuffed them back in the bag and tossed them out the window in the general direction of a dumpster. Then each Puerto Rican fired up a cigarette as Diego fired up the van. As we pulled out onto the road and began driving back to the shop, the van filled with smoke because there were no windows in the back and those in the front were mostly closed.

"It's, uh, getting a little smokey back here," I said over the echoing whirr of the engine.

"Here," Hector growled, handing me a cigarette and his lighter. "Helps the buzz."

"Oh, I uh," began to explain what I really meant, but an impatient Hector thrust them harder in my direction so I corrected myself: "Oh, thanks!" With the buzz I had going, I rationalized this as being as good a time as any to try my first one. And, as it turned out, he was right.

There was a long stretch of time that summer where I worked with Jerry every day. Each morning we'd climb into his truck and he'd tip that Alvin the Chipmunk hat skyward and peer around to see if anyone was looking. When the coast was clear he'd looked at me with sheepish eyes. "Do you want a hit of..." he'd trail off to sneak another peek around for onlookers before whispering, "*weeed?*"

"Uhhh, yah," I'd say in my best isn't-it-obvious tone. Sometimes I'd mix things up—"Why that'd be lovely, Jerald!"—or occasionally decline just to see him flash disappointment before admitting it was a gag. "*Of course* I wanna get high with you," I'd say, much to his relief.

Jerry was only good for only one hit himself, though. "Just enough to enjoy work, heyy!"

He had this peculiar tic, unbeknownst to him, where he'd sprinkle the word "heyy" throughout his speech.

"Whatcha got for lunch, heyy?"

"That's nice work, heyy!"

"Whadda ya say, heyy?"

It got annoying at times, but it was always followed by this boyish grin, so you couldn't hate him for it. In fact, Jerry was really a boy trapped in an old man's frame. His body aged, but his mind remained as chipper as a teen's. He enjoyed playing basketball until he could hardly walk, whiffle-ball until he threw his back out, and throwing rocks at anything or anyone he felt deserved it until his arm gave way—all while on the clock, I might add. This endless abundance of energy was because Jerry had discovered the fountain of youth.

I believe it was the early onset of a chronic cocaine habit that sealed Jerry's adolescent mindset in time. I was rewarded with a laundry list of items when I asked him what other drugs he'd tried. It's no wonder his experimentation was responsible for his being sacked from the first real job he had as a young man: Big-time Drug Dealer. A few years in prison seemed like a slap on the wrist for the stories he told me. He used to run shipments from Miami up north, fucking stewardesses and blowing lines with politicians on the way. I was never surprised when we drove by a university staff member or construction worker on the job site and he'd point his finger and giggle, "I do coke with that guy." Then he'd wave to his drug buddy as we drove by, aimlessly circling around campus to look busy.

The last time I saw Jerry was less than a month after I'd left school. I went back to the shop to visit my friends and approached Jerry with a smile and an outstretched hand. He shook it firmly with a grin on his face that expressed his happiness to see me.

"Heyy," he said with that boyish grin. And then, "I'm Jerry!"

I paused, staring at him. "Jerry," I muttered, "it's me."

He plowed over that statement and told me, "You remind me of a kid that used to work here, heyy!"

"Yeah, Jerry, it's me. That was a few weeks ago."

"Nahhh, I'm talkin' *way* back, heyy."

At a loss for words, I stood frozen like Bill Murray on the first morning of *Groundhog Day*. We spent many days together that summer, but the weed and coke had already erased me from his mind.

"Nice to meet ya, heyy!" he told me as he walked away.

Jerry had once said to me, "I used to do everything on everything," when asked if he'd ever tried adderall and weed while skiing. And it's looking back now, remembering that boyish grin forever glued to his face, that I think I made the right choice in getting sober. The thrills of slicing through trees with friends on drugs will forever be etched in my mind, but I'd also like to remember new friends for more than a month at a time.

THE HOARDER

"But I don't want to go among mad people," Alice remarked.
"Oh, you can't help that," said the Cat:
"we're all mad here. I'm mad. You're mad."
"How do you know I'm mad?" said Alice.
"You must be," said the Cat,
"or you wouldn't have come here."
—Lewis Carroll, Alice in Wonderland

"Thanks for finding a place to stay," Jack told me as we took our bags from the trunk.

"Figured I'd give AirBnB a try," I said, neither of us having much travel experience just two years after school.

The sun hung low in the California sky as we stepped foot onto a driveway of rough handiwork. An odd mixture of cobblestone, brick, rocks, and other collections led the way toward a borderline rundown home.

"Is this," Jack began, pausing to blink at a small sheet of plywood covering what was presumably a hole in the roof, "it..?"

An overgrowth of palms hid some of the one-story home from view, but the bent and mangled overhang jutting out over the door could be seen clearly. Wood-carved animals, a giant rainbow umbrella, and an old bathtub were among an assortment of other junk that decorated the front "porch," if that's how you could even describe it. It was a pleasant junkyard, really. The aging wooden exterior of the home left it a smidge shy of ramshackle at best.

"Right address," I shrugged.

We walked toward a decrepit work shed halfway up the scattered path. Clamorous sounds poured out from inside. Jack tapped my arm and gestured off toward a naked statue laced in Mardi Gras beads. A few steps later, I returned the favor, pointing to an ornamental flamingo that sat at the base of a manikin's head, stuck on a pike with blood-like paint streaming down its face.

"Well," said Jack, frowning his disappointment, "ya done good." Those were the words that came out of his mouth, but "ya fucked us" is what he meant. "Should we go now before it's too la—"

Jack was cut short as a small and mangy furball burst through the door of the shed, yapping wildly.

"What're ye barkin' at?" a voice emerged from inside. Then an older man with crazy brown hair poked his head out the door. He saw us standing there as he emerged from the shed wearing a Hawaiian shirt and tattered jeans. "Don' you worry," said the man, "he won' hur'cha." He scratched his balls with one hand while in the other he held a butcher's knife. With a smile, he pointed the knife our way and said, "You mus' be my guests!"

"Uhh, y-yes," I said. "I believe we exchanged some texts about a room with two beds?"

"Bunkbeds! To be exact," said the man.

"*Bunk* beds..?" said Jack.

"Built 'em myself!" said the man. "Come on in, boys. I'll show ya." And with that, he swung his knife in a follow-me sort of way and marched up the cobble-brick-stone driveway. He disappeared under the makeshift overhang trimmed with wind chimes, pinwheels, and roadsigns.

"After you," I told Jack, giving him a gentle nudge in the man's direction.

"*Bunk* beds?" said Jack as he began walking. "What are we, boy scouts?"

"That detail wasn't mentioned in the profile," I said. "But I already paid. Let's at least check it out."

He rolled his eyes as he followed the plump little mutt skittering behind the man's trail. "He's gonna feed us to that dog. You know that, don't you?"

"Or the plants," I said, nodding toward a slew of Venus flytraps encircling a swampy fountain.

We followed the man through a bright yellow door into a dimly lit room. An aviation suit and oxygen mask from WWII hung as the centerpiece on the far wall. Beneath it stood a dusty bookshelf, patched together with mismatched wooden planks. On the shelves were an assortment of clown figurines.

"You're welcome to use the kitchen," said the man, slapping his knife on top of the fridge so it dangled over the edge precariously. Every inch of the fridge was covered in a hodgepodge of magnets and stickers. The cabinets were turquoise, the support beams purple, the ceiling orange. He led us by a teal ladder and patted the wooden railing, saying, "If you only needed one bed, ya coulda had the loft!"

"Oh darn," said Jack, staring me down. "If only…"

"Built that as well," bragged the man.

"Um, lovely place you've got here," I lied as we followed him down a hall. "I'm surprised you don't, uh, highlight your profile with more, you know, *enlightening* photos."

The man stopped in front of a stained curtain in place of where a door used to be. "Here's the bathroom," said the man, yanking it back to reveal the inside. "There's only one, so make it quick." He paused for a moment as a thought popped into his head. "Oh! Important rule," he snapped his fingers: "Boys pee in the backyard." There was an awkward pause before he said, "There's a drought here in California." Then he wagged his finger back and forth between us and added, "Gotta do our part to save water."

"Perfect," said Jack. "I *prefer* to use the yard!"

"Here's your room," said the man, leading us to a dank and musty space with the promised bunks.

"Dee-lightful," said Jack, tossing his bag on a decrepit rocking chair in the corner. "We love it!"

"I hate housework," said the man. "You make the beds, you do the dishes, and six months later you have to start all over!" He gave us a smile and added, "Joan Rivers. Ha!" Then he closed the door behind him, and we heard him go back outside.

"At least this room has a door," said Jack, shaking his head with a sigh.

"And posters," I said, pointing at the wall with a smile.

Jack looked up to see the vintage cover of Greg Randolph's risqué and erotic fiction novel, *Sex Goddess,* hanging on the wall. Next to it was a poster of Dr. Seuss with the quote, "Be who you are and say what you feel, because those who mind don't matter and those who matter don't mind!"

"How do *you* feel?" I asked.

"Scared or starving," said Jack. "Take your pick."

"Same," I said. "Downtown is a short walk from here."

"Let's go," said Jack.

As we left the house and walked past the sounds of tinkering in the work shed Jack whispered, "I bet that's where he keeps the meat grinder."

I slapped him on the back and said, "I'm sure we'll find out later."

"I hate you so much," he told me.

Then a cool darkness fell as we walked downtown.

~ ~ ~

Upon our return, we found our host with an older couple, crowded around the only small folding table the living room had to offer. Their business casual attire had them looking out of place, eating from unmatched platters and drinking from unmatched glasses. I felt sensitive to the tingle of familiarity that filled the air between them. As we entered the room with our outsiders' vibe, it mixed with their intimate affair like oil in water.

"Heree theyy aree," announced the man with a tipsy gusto. "I was just telli—[a *hiccup* interrupted his speech]—my friends what wonderful guests you are. Not a *peep* from you boys!" The woman gave us a friendly smile, welcoming enough I supposed, but her husband sat to himself with a neutral air, either unfazed by our intrusion or too drunk to care.

I was leery of getting sucked into a formal introduction followed by an invitation to pull up more chairs around a space that already struggled to squeeze three. I planned to cut this exchange short by telling the man we had stepped out for a quick bite to eat, but that we must promptly retire so we can get far, far away from this dump as early as possible. I opened my mouth to do so when Jack pointed to our host's legs and said, "Those are interesting pajamas."

A strange silence fell over the room as all eyes shifted toward the man's evening attire. As much as I despised Jack for engaging in conversation, he made a good point. It became apparent our host was wearing children's patterned pajamas. But not just any pajamas; this pair—or pairs, as it turned out to be— were two different styles of children's pajamas sewn together at the knees. One pattern ran the length of his thighs and the other down to his ankles. I tried to suppress the notion of sleeping in the bunks of two children buried in the backyard and peeing on them later that night.

"Aren't they!?" said the woman, breaking the tension by patting our host on the knee. "He's so *resourceful*," she added with what I thought was an interesting choice of words. "He's built half this house himself you know!"

This woman was clearly in cahoots with this psychopath. Not to mention her husband was yet to make eye contact, probably out of guilt with what his loony bin associates were up to.

"Yup!" said the man. "This wholeee room is made of materi—[*hiccup*]—al I fetched from *dumpsters*." He continued on by slurring, "Down to the las—[*hiccup*]—nail." Then he added a prideful wink of an eye.

"Is that... legal?" said Jack, peering around the room, eventually fixing his gaze upon the glass the woman raised to her lips.

Legal? I thought. *Legal!? Does whittling down the bones of children to make nails sound legal to you?*

"Wellll, mos' of the wiring has been inspected," slurred the man. "I'm sure the res' is up to—[*hiccup*]—code."

"Ah, yes," said Jack. "Up to code." Then he elbowed me discreetly before asking, "Did you say you built our beds as well?"

"Sure did!" said the man. "Sturdy as a—[*hiccup*]—horse."

"*Dumpster* horse," Jack coughed into his hand only loud enough for me to hear.

"Well, we're pretty tired from all the driving," I said.

"Sure you boys don't want a glass of wine?" said the woman, quivering her plastic mug like a bell.

"Ooo," Jack encouraged me. "Glass of wine!?"

"Oh no, no," I chuckled, privy to whatever that murderous witch had brewed. "We really shouldn't. We've got a such early start in the morning."

"Next time you're in town then!" said the man, punching his own Disney cup in the sky, splashing his drink onto one of the two half-carpets that had been stitched together as one.

"Certainly!" said Jack, pumping his fist hooray. "We'll be back *real* soon!"

"You fellas—[*hiccup*]—are welcome anytime," said the man.

With that we thanked him and bid the couple goodnight then fled to our room. Jack closed the door and with a stark shift in demeanor said, "Did you even *look* at the reviews?"

"In my defense," I said, "no one mentioned getting murdered."

"Show me," he said, rummaging through his bag for a toothbrush.

I searched for my own as I flipped through the phone to find the man's profile.

"Well, in hindsight—"

"And you've got 20/20," said Jack, leaving the room and walking down the hall. I followed behind as he stepped past the stained bathroom curtain. A row of rubber ducklings lined the top of the toilet, swimming amongst what appeared to be driblets of fecal matter. Jack pointed this out as he pressed on. "You were saying?"

"I'm noticing a few, well," I paused to roll my hand in search of the right word, "giveaways." Then I read the tidbits of different descriptions aloud. "'*Eclectic,*' '*unique,*' '*open-minded,*' '*an artful masterpiece,*' and, oh, here's a good one, '*a carnival of sensory experiences.*' Must've missed that one."

"Real nice, man," said Jack as the sounds of the guests leaving drifted down the hall. We heard the host retire and the house fell silent.

"Ah, this one definitely slipped through the cracks," I said. "'*This house is like a museum. It's hoarded, which means it's unsanitary. A full crew couldn't clean around a thousand objects. When I checked in he tried to give me a hug and touched my lower back as he led me to the bedroom. I found a used tissue next to my pillow. I got three bites from spiders and bugs and had nightmares of an insect invasion and him creeping into my room.*'"

When I finished reading the review, I looked up to see Jack frozen, mid-brush, staring toward the upper corner of the mirror. I followed his gaze and caught the reflection of a small shelf nailed to the wall by the ceiling. Staring back at us were three dolls. Well, the heads of three dolls anyway.

There was a long and awkward pause before Jack mumbled something like, "Well that's unsettling," with the toothbrush still dangling from his lips.

"Do you mean the missing bodies," I said, "or the nightmares of a creeping rapist?"

He spat abruptly into the sink and left me with the fecal ducks and corpse-less dolls.

When I returned to the room, he was lying on the top bunk with his shoes still on. Despite the warm temperature, he had put on a hooded sweatshirt to spare his head from contact with a pillow he must have assumed was also fetched from the trash.

"If the rusty screws fail," said Jack, staring off into the ceiling with his fingers laced over his chest, "you should be the one to get crushed."

"And spare me from being raped and fed to the dog?" I said. "What a guy!"

He told me to go fuck myself and with that I turned off the lights. As he heard me settle atop my own dusty quilt he asked, "How's that dumpster mattress?"

"Crusted by the fluids of a necrophiliac, no doubt."

"Sweet dreams, asshole."

"Love you too, man."

We both fell silent. Not a toss in fear of stirring the bed lice, not a turn in fear of collapsing the erection of garbage.

An hour of silence passed before Jack said, "You awake?"

"Uh, yah."

"Wanna get the fuck outta here?"

"Uh, yah."

We grabbed our bags and crept into the wee hours of the morning, the descending moon the only witness of our escape. Once in the safety of the car, Jack said, "I think I'll choose where we stay next time." And with that, we fled the scene.

NUDE BEACH

I imagine there are two types of people out there: those who are comfortable at a nude beach, and the other 99.9% of humanity. I had a hunch I didn't belong to the small minority, but I wanted to make sure, so I took a little field trip out of curiosity.

Before I carry on, let me pop in a quick disclaimer for the prudes and puritans.

DISCLAIMER: This story is not for the prudes and puritans.

Now that that's settled let's carry on.

The first and only time I went to Florida's first and only legal clothing optional beach was sometime after college and before adulthood. An age where "finding yourself"-type insecurities fuel your judgments of, and comparisons to, others. A place in life where a well-hung black man strolling toward you with a half-dollar-sized hoop pierced through his cock might cause you to blink twice, for example. (Should I stick a second disclaimer here to let you know it gets worse? Or have I already fried your

82

brain beyond repair?) Nothing lets a young man know where he stands in the sexual marketplace quite like a well-endowed, Schwarzenegger-like figure strolling down the sand with his jewelry swaying in the wind.

Not everyone's body looked this way, though. In fact, most bodies weren't doing much strolling or swaying at all. More like plodding, trudging, slogging, drooping, flapping, sagging, or any other verbs that portray the antithesis of the *Baywatch* scene I was hoping for.

This quarter-mile stretch of Haulover Beach is separated from the rest of the park with a sign. For anyone privileged enough with literacy, it warns, **ATTENTION**: BEYOND THIS POINT YOU MAY ENCOUNTER NUDE BATHERS. I realized far too late that it was further divided by a change in demographic somewhere around the halfway mark—the north populated by gays, the south by non-gays. That isn't to say there's a line in the sand where a bouncer checks your sexual orientation at the door. ("Queer? Come on through! Hetero? Why don't you take a hike southbound, *buddy*.") It's more like somewhere between lifeguard chairs there's an unspoken rule that if you fancy the same gender, you stick to one side, and if you prefer the opposite, well then you stick to the opposite.

I had chosen a spacious plot somewhere in the middle—no man's land, or the best of both worlds one might say. To my left were creepy old gay guys, glancing in my direction as they performed either pilates or some kind of mating ritual. To my right were creepy old straight guys who parked themselves a sniff away from the women sunbathing, making sure they had a prime view before groping themselves without invitation. Despite the rules discouraging such lewd behavior, there seemed to be a high tolerance for it judging by the lack of anyone I saw patrolling these sands. Who can blame them, though: I didn't want the role of Pervert Police on my resume either.

There's no way to play it cool at a nude beach. You're either one of the weirdos flaunting everything or you're one of the outcasts with clothes on. Either way it's uncomfortable, either way it's a lose-lose. The only winners in this kind of place are the gawkers, one such being who swaggered over by me and jiggled out of a SPEEDO a little too close by.

This Santa-like creature managed to shimmy off its clothes before they ripped at the seams. Then it dumped its jolly ass down facing me, not the ocean, as is the quietly agreed upon protocol at the beach. I watched the eyes of this thing wander in both directions, though, which is when I realized my staked middle ground might be for bisexuals, or at least those curious by nature. Whenever those eyes drifted toward me I would make as if swatting a fly away and think as loud as I could, *Beat it, Santa!*—soon after realizing my poor choice of words.

I suppose this might be how women feel throughout most of their lives: flattered to some degree, but also wishing you could turn it off. There should be a requirement at the nude beach that everyone wear sunglasses, regardless of clouds or time of day. We don't need to confirm whether or not your eyes are drifting toward our assholes; at least *pretend* you're looking past us toward the waves. And I know this is a place where most rules go out the window, but your hands shouldn't be in your nether regions for more than three seconds at a time. If you've got an itch, that's one thing. Or if you need to flip your "self" over to ensure an even tan, that's another. And we understand these are delicate areas, but sunscreen doesn't need to be applied *that* often.

Here's when a fantasy stung my mind: What if my hat blew off and started rolling down the shore? Would I chase after it, bending over every time a gust of wind blew it further? Or would I let it go and risk getting skin cancer? The cancer seemed less painful than chancing a drive-by sodomization by Father Time.

I felt bad for the kid with the job of dragging beach chairs and setting up umbrellas for these characters. It's like, Dude, is $9 an hour really worth scarring yourself for the rest of your life? This poor guy set up one snobby couple—with snapping fingers and no tip—and as soon as they sat down, the woman took out a giant bag of Smart Food popcorn. Is Smart Food really a smart choice at a nude beach, with that powdery cheese crumbling into your bellybutton, brewing a sweaty goo that flows over like a volcano? Couldn't you go with pretzels, or something with a bit less residue? It's bad enough this kid has to wipe down greasy perspirations that already resemble curds and whey, but now he has to scrub away your actual cheese remnants as well? Is it me or is courtesy a thing of the past?

I watched this woman struggle mercilessly to open her bag. With a sudden explosion, her chair collapsed, and popcorn came raining down everywhere. Let me tell you: You don't feel more embarrassment for someone than you do watching them fall into the sand naked, cheesy body parts jiggling as gravity claims their behind. She was a Smart Food fool as far as I was concerned, and she brought this upon herself. I glanced around to see if anyone else witnessed this train wreck when I locked eyes with good Ol' Saint Nick, still rubbing away with the confidence of a true creeper. That's when I flipped Santa the bird and told him to put me on his naughty list as I packed up to leave. It began raining, you see, and the only other option was to huddle under the cabanas with the perverted geezers. I appreciate a fair amount of personal space in clothed settings, so squeezing in with a hodgepodge of nudists didn't feel like my scene.

I was almost back at the parking lot when a quick shift in Miami weather brought the sunshine around again. I hesitated over wasting the money I'd already paid for parking and decided to venture back to the predominantly straight part of the beach this time around. There wasn't as much excitement to report there. A lot of what resembled a community sponge bath at a retirement home: droopy old ladies to whom gravity had been unkind, pot-bellied men who hadn't seen their own dicks in ages. I did see Mr. Cock Piercing playfully splashing about with two Latinas, so that was exciting. But other than that, things were as quiet and awkward as I imagine the nude beach tends to be, with more and more people filing out as the evening cool rolled in.

This dip in the action lasted until the lifeguards got off duty, at which point—I shit you not (and this is where the disclaimer really kicks in)—the beach divides into two more schools: exhibitionists and voyeurs. That's right, I mean you're either gettin' down or you're watchin' others get down. And if you're not pickin' up what I'm puttin' down, I mean they're fuckin', right there on the beach. Does that help clarify what my shy and awkward self was experiencing?

I must have missed the paragraph describing this sundown ritual on the state park website. There, Haulover was described as somewhere families can play, not somewhere families are made. But there I was, witnessing the latter.

I didn't notice this shift in activity until I watched a man abruptly pick up his beach chair by the arms and scurry closer to a couple embracing passionately on a towel nearby. There he plunked down his chair, dropped his shorts, and began masturbating vigorously. The couple didn't seem to mind. In fact, at this point I gathered they were there for that sort of thing.

That's about the time I decided the nude beach wasn't for me. God forbid I was found by some police officer who finally decided to do his job, questioning my involvement in the scene. *How good would **that** mark look on my record?* I wondered.

And so I discovered the nude beach wasn't volleyball courts of models and tight bosoms like I'd hoped for. There were no sexy lifeguards jogging down the beach in slow motion and even fewer nude yoga sessions with the world's finest yogis (unless you count the Pilates-mating rituals, which I personally would not). Instead, it turned out to be a cramped strip of land filled with bodies you'd never otherwise see in explicit films or a sexy TV series.

And look, I understand it takes balls to be naked in front of strangers. (Saggy, wrinkled, ancient balls that shoot dust upon orgasm, but balls nonetheless.) So if you're planning a trip to a nude beach anytime soon, don't let my story dissuade you. Just make sure to rub sunscreen on your eyes, in addition to your ghostly colored privates, as they're equally as likely to burn.

And who knows. Perhaps one day I'll get over my insecurities and you'll find me a part of the geriatric circus, but for now I'll remain a prude and stick to the puritans' beaches.

KETOZONE

*"The moment there is suspicion
about a person's motives,
everything he does
becomes tainted."*
—*Mahatma Gandhi*

Now I have a degree in Exercise Science from one of the top research institutions in the country, so I've acquired my fair share of knowledge regarding sports nutrition. I drop this subtle brag upon you only to say that it'd be difficult to pull a fast one on me in this realm. That's something the sales rep from a company we'll call Ketozone didn't know when she walked into my personal training studio one afternoon.

Ketozone, she claimed, was a proud revolutionary in the world of supplementation. By simply consuming their exogenous ketones once a day, you can skirt the strict and necessary sacrifice of carbs it normally takes to enjoy the benefits of a Ketogenic Diet! Typically, only by depriving the body of any sugars for an extended stretch of days or weeks can you tap into the fat loss, improved cholesterol, lower blood pressure, clarity of mind, and a boost in overall mood and energy levels touted by the practitioners of the diet. But no longer! Why adhere to those pesky restrictions when you can merely tear open a packet of ketones and pour them into a bottle of water once to twice per day and—voilà—ketosis is yours for the taking!

I was quite familiar with the world of supplement research and had yet to hear anything about this revolution, so naturally I was intrigued. I asked this peppy young representative a few probing questions about the science behind how her supplement worked, to which she answered excitedly.

"For anyone who discovers the benefits of Ketozone," she told me, "they are encouraged to join their team as a representative!" And by inspiring others with my success story, I would not only be saving the world with this revolutionary health solution but also receiving a commission on every sale! Additionally, if I were to recruit other representatives, I'd receive a piece of *their* commission as well! And get this: It doesn't stop there! Because I'd also receive a cut of anyone's commission under *that* recruiter as wel—

"Yeah, but how does it actually, you know, *work*?" I asked. "Do you have some studies?"

Unfortunately, this young gunner hadn't brought any studies with her, nor did she know the science off the top of her head. "But!" she told me. "I can connect you with the most knowledgeable person I know in the Ketozone community." I was assured that this "top income earner" would answer all my questions. Then, as sure as the rising sun, he'd pave my way to a six-figure salary in no time. All I had to do was work hard and abide by the company motto: "Get out there and *prove it!*"

Prove what, exactly? I wondered.

A Facebook Messenger invite was extended my way later that evening. The Keto Oracle began by comforting me with an extended list of his credentials, comprised mostly of having "literally met, interviewed, *and* talked to the top Ketogenic researchers in the world."

Thoroughly impressed, I asked about Ketozone's claim that consuming their product can put anyone into ketosis without actually abiding by a strict Ketogenic Diet. I requested a link to the body of scientific evidence showing they can achieve in seconds what typically requires anywhere from days and weeks to achieve.

I was ignored on repeated requests for this evidence throughout our exchange. Instead, he pitched curveballs of BroScience as I caught ever more puzzling statements regarding their mysterious powder. I was told the body of unprovided research is "hundreds of years old," yet, in a later statement, he revealed that Ketozone was only two and a half years old. No mind need be paid to that insignificant time gap, though, because fortunately they "never have to actually test their products because they work every single time in every single person." I could only assume this claim was passed down by his scientific bro pals, whom he'd literally met, interviewed, *and* talked to.

He went on to tell me that unfortunately, the average person will never have elevated blood ketone levels without the consumption of their product, and "they absolutely *need* them!" I found this a powerful statement from a company that neglected to provide a single piece of supporting evidence, not to mention the billions of folks who've gotten by just fine without them in the prior millennium. But what did I know, as someone who's never literally met, interviewed, *and* talked to these scientists.

Even if I were able to wrap my feeble mind around this one hundred (or only two-and-a-half)-year-old body of research, I was surprised to find out it wasn't actually available to the general public anyway. "The evidence you're looking for," I was told, "is only revealed at our conferences." Tickets to, say, the upcoming Vegas convention usually cost $1,000, but for the measly fee of $500, this generous soul offered to sneak me in. However! Time was of the essence, and he could only offer me this deal if I transferred him the money for my plane ticket and five-day hotel stay—Right. Now.

"I'm devastated," I told him. "I'm getting an oil change that day."

I asked if there was any available information regarding his product whatsoever, but any further inquiries were cut short because he was "a very busy man" and "we could go on forever about it." He concluded by assuring me he's "already spoken to these men" and this council of nameless scientists has justified his claim of how effective his product would be for every one of my personal training clients. If I wanted to discuss the matter any further, I'd have to join him later that night at the Ketozone social mixer, conveniently located nearby.

"Conjure magic for them and they'll be distracted."
—*Gracchus, Gladiator*

I prefer live entertainment over television when I can get it, so I arrived at the mixer fashionably late and slipped through the door of a small conference room. There, I made my way to the back of the room where I could get a good view. Already, there was a crowd of around thirty people—varying in shape, size, gender, and age—most of whom were holding a glass filled with a neon pink liquid resembling Kool-Aid. They sat in chairs, on couches, or leaned against walls, all facing the one woman standing at the center of attention.

A form-fitting dress hugged her athletic curves as she confidently delivered the tail-end of a well-rehearsed speech.

There was a round of applause before she said, "And now I'd like to call upon a few of our newer members to talk about their experience with Ketozone!"

It quickly appeared as though everyone who was part of the organization had a success story to tell—a downward spiraling tale turned upright by joining the all-powerful Ketozone team. A number of valued members were "put on the spot" to share their personal stories. One by one, they would feign a blush and sheepishly step up to the front of the room. Their tale would begin with a bashful statement like, "Wow, I, uh, didn't expect to be called up here like this. I'm, uh, a bit shy, but here it goes." Then they'd rip into a thoughtfully-crafted journey, powerful enough to compel any listener to buy some product immediately if not sooner.

One poor soul slumped up to the front of the room and tried his darnedest to hold back a tear. After a dramatic pause to dab his eyes with a tissue, he broke the grievous tension with an Alcoholics Anonymous tone. "Hello. My name is Jerry, and I used to consume at least three energy drinks a day."

I was expecting a greeting in unison—"Hi Jerry!"—but instead, there was well-practiced concern glued to every rep's face, regardless of surely having heard this yarn a thousand times.

"At more than $3 a drink," Jerry pushed forth, "it was costing me a *fortune!*" Then his demeanor turned to an uplifting charm. "But since discovering Ketozone, I've been able to kick that expensive habit by supplementing with just *three* servings of ketones a day!" And as if straight out of an infomercial, he pulled out some product from nowhere and raised it for all to see. "This is one of Ketozone's multiple flavors, enhanced with enough caffeine to out-perform a cup of coffee!" There was an eruption of applause from his fellow supporters as he concluded with a greasy, car-salesman's smile. "And I've never felt better!"

Unable to stand a moment more of this nonsensical drivel, I silenced the crowd with an over-exaggerated slow-clap and sauntered to the front of the room. "Now wasn't that just *peachy,*" I chuckled with a final, echoing clap. An awkward tension putrefied the air as all eyes followed my violation of the man's personal space. "Well done there, Mister *Jerry,* is it?" I threw my arm around his shoulder and turned us both to face the room as I pressed on. "Lemme ask ya somethin' there, Jer."

"Uh, yes?" he squeaked in nervous confusion.

I paused to scan the crowd then turned to look Jerry deep into his fraudulent eyes. "So what you're saying is that you kicked the habit of drinking three *caffeinated* energy drinks a day, costing three dollars each, by replacing them with three *caffeinated* Ketozone drinks, costing six dollars each, to spare yourself the financial burden of a *caffeinated* beverage addiction..?"

My arm fell from Jerry's shoulder as I threw them out wide, ambling toward the crowd. "My good people," I said, adopting my best impersonation of Russell Crowe. "Are you not entertained!?"

Alright, maybe I made that last bit up, but clearly no one applied simple mathematics to calculate the load of bullshit this man was shoveling down their throats. Back in reality, everyone was clapping for Jerry as he took his seat, so I bit my lip and scrounged for a single tear myself to honor his bravery.

The speaker who followed Jerry was a thin, jittery woman with an infant strapped to her chest. She rhythmically bounced the babe for the entirety of her speech. This tear-jerker began to unfold as if she was reading cue cards somewhere in the back of the room. She vented a past suffering through low energy and a struggle to find consistent income. In short, she found this company right after getting pregnant, and now, working for and consuming Ketozone full-time, she's alleviated both her financial and energetic burden.

"I no longer have to worry about being a single mother," she preached. Then she turned the attention of her story toward her child. "All babies are born into a state of ketosis you know."

Interesting, I thought. *Never considered that.*

"But my baby will remain a Keto-baby—"

Go on...

"—with the help of—"

Please don't say...

"Ketozone!"

What!? I stared in disbelief. *Does Child Services concern themselves with feeding infants unregulated supplements?*

"Because," she went on, "I like to mix half a packet of ketones into a bottle of—"

She's not about to say...

"—breastmilk!" She hoisted a pink bottle into the air and an eruption of applause ensued.

*Well, **that** parental decision seems a tad surprising,* I thought, realizing as she walked off stage to kiss her husband that this was the wife of the Keto Oracle himself, breeding a Keto army.

When I snapped out of shock and realized I was the only one not clapping again, I quickly punched a fist in the air in a manner I hoped conveyed, "You *go* girl!"

Pity-time closed with a finale of ever more ridiculous miracles like Mister "One day at the corporate water cooler I felt

I'd become a new man and quit my job to sell ketones" and Miss "The pounds just melted away without any dietary or lifestyle changes whatsoever!"

"Be careful of those who offer you a cashmere sweater while they slowly pull the wool over your eyes."
—Linda Poindexter

"I'm so glad you made it!" a voice fluttered into my ear as the meeting came to an end. "Here," the Keto Oracle greeted me with an outstretched cup of pink liquid in his hand. "Try this."

"It's an absolute pleasure," I lied, exchanging the drink for a handshake.

He stood a proud six feet tall, chest pumped by more dumbbell flyes than any man should perform in a lifetime. A pair of skinny jeans revealed a disproportionate interest in achieving similar gains below the belt. When he spoke, he retracted only his shoulder blades, never his unwavering beliefs.

"You're gonna have a promising career here at Ketozone," he assumed. "Joining the family will be the best decision of your life." Then, he carried on more assertively. "You're sharp, very knowledgeable."

"Why thank yo—"

"We could use someone like you on this team."

"Well I still don't kno—"

"I used to be a trainer just like you, scrounging for clients, struggling to pay bills, lacking so much as a car."

"Actually, I drove her—"

"That's all behind us now!" he yelled. He wrapped one arm around my shoulders as he said, "Soon you'll be like me." With the other he scanned the horizon and said, "Big house, nice car, beautiful woman, and feeling *fannn*-tastic!" He pointed toward the untouched cup in my hand and said, "And we owe it all to those ketones." Then, with some uninvited assistance, he helped lift the drink to my face and suggested again that I try some.

"Ahh," I sipped. "Heavenly."

"Of course they are!" he said. "And they'll change your life forever. Working for Ketozone has become a dream..." he trailed off in reverie. "Then again, is this *really* even working?"

"So how does Ketoz—"

"Drink up!" he plowed through me again. "Then we'll getcha another flavor." I complied and gulped down the last half-glass, realizing the slim chance of slipping another word in. He topped me off with another iridescent liquid the color of which could never be found in nature.

They are tasty, I thought, giving way to the monologue. *I'll give him that much.*

He yammered on with a warm and mesmerizing gaze as he lead me through a slew of flavor samples. My thoughts gave way to the sound of his voice and the colorful potions, the combination unraveling my wall of skepticism and leaving me defenseless. I tuned in and out of his words, bobble-heading through the palatable cosmos of my own consciousness.

[...a sip of Rasberry...]
"...and so our company is like Apple..."
...mhmm, like Apple...

[...lulled by Lemonade...]
"...everyone wishes they bought stock back then..."
...shoulda bought stock back then...

[...rapt in Maui Punch...]
"...you need investments in your life..."
...investments in my life...

[...charmed by Chocolate Swirl...]
"...and make a career for yourself..."
...career for myself...

[...in an Orange Dream...]
"...all from your phone..."
... all from my pho—

[*DING!*]

His own phone rang. He ripped it out of his jeans, and with a finger-snap to an exuberant handgun, he yelled, "Look at that! I've made money just standing here!" He snapped me right out of the daze and advised that I "Stop wasting time and start earning money! Right. Now."

Like a hypnotized victim told to act like a duck, I quacked, "Right. Now." Then I whipped out my card to have a hundred and thirty bucks plucked from my account for a box of Maui Punch.

> *"When people leave cults,*
> *they don't know that they left a cult."*
> —Sean Durkin

"I think I just left a cult," I muttered to myself on the drive home.

I finished the product within a month of the hypnosis and felt absolutely nothing at all. I contacted the all-knowing Oracle to pick his brain on how to get my money back. I told him I expected to feel *something* for a hundred and thirty dollars, especially based on the testimonials of life-changing improvements. Apparently, "that's irrelevant" and it's "very important" to drink the product "twice a day every day" for benefits that "we're not going to feel." At least that's what I gathered from the best response The Oracle could muster. He was finally kind enough to direct me to the Ketozone.com/research webpage before avalanching down another rabbit hole of BroScience malarkey.

There, I combed through their website thoroughly and discovered a few enlightening tidbits of information. Before linking to any research, the site itself clarifies, "Under no circumstance is the information contained within such third party research to be used or considered as a direct, or indirect study of any Ketozone product." From there each ensuing link goes on to reference studies performed on Ketogenic *Diets,* not exogenous ketone products. One referenced study was actually conducted by a former college professor of mine stating, "There needs to be more studies performed on exogenous ketones." The Ketozone website even suggests their product be used to complement a Ketogenic Diet with the addition of exercise. These variables are scientifically proven to have benefits *without* the addition of exogenous ketones, so Ketozone was piggybacking off and printing the claims right on the box as their own.

No one I talked to at Ketozone could show me any real evidence their product actually does anything. My final chat with The Oracle included statements such as, "You won't feel any benefits because you're already feeling healthy" and how "it's necessary to come to the Ketozone conferences [read: spend more money] and take 5-6 packets a day [read: 2-3x the recommended dose] to feel any real difference [read: to become a recruiter for my Multi-level Marketing scheme]." My last question for The Oracle before we never spoke again was whether or not it'd be more efficient to just wheel around an IV of ketones everywhere you go.

When I spoke to the first young lady later on, she informed me that, "I myself don't agree with everything he said. Like taking two ketones a day? That's over $400 a month!" And even more surprising, she went on to contradict their company motto by admitting, "I struggle to show it works myself because there's no evidence to, you know, actually *prove it*."

JUST MY LUCK

"I love the DMV!
Can I go with you?"
said no one ever.
—Random Meme

I've lived in Connecticut, California, Florida, Massachusetts, Colorado, and Connecticut and Florida again, which means I've been to the DMV in Connecticut, California, Florida, Massachusetts, Colorado, and Connecticut and Florida again. Let me tell you how wonderful those experiences have been by combining these stories into one collective DMV tale in a fictional state pronounced Cal-nnect-ass-ori-do.

Ever since COVID, you have to book an appointment at the DMV. In theory, this was the smartest thing they'd ever done. In reality, though, the soonest available appointment is no less than one month in the future, which directly contradicts the website of most states where they say if you don't register your car within ten days of becoming a resident, you're apt to receive some kind of enormous fine.

On the day of my appointment, I took two hours of vacation time off work assuming that was enough for a midday errand. I arrived to find the parking lot nearly jam-packed, but fortunately, there was a man in a safety vest to point out an empty space in case I was blind.

"Thank God you're here!" I didn't say as he told me to roll down the window.

Safety man asked, "Do you know how to back into a space?"

Do I know how to back into a space? I thought, wondering how many of my tax dollars this guy was being paid to ask me such a thing. "Of course," I said politely.

"Good," he said, doubling down on the old pointing routine.

I desperately wanted to know what happened if I couldn't, but I didn't ask.

I arrived ten minutes before my appointment, as instructed, to find a line stretching out the door, down and around the wheelchair ramp, along the length of the building, and around the corner. I walked up to the guy at the door with a clipboard checking people in and told him my appointment number. Clipboard man confirmed that I was indeed at the right place, in case I was blind, then he told me to wait at the end of the line.

"I think there's some confusion," I said. "I have *an appointment.*"

"You and everybody else, pal," said clipboard man as a fellow appointment-setter stepped behind me to check in. As I craned my neck to look down the disappearing line he shouted, "Next!" right into my ear. And so I slumped to the back of the line like a good little boy.

I slugged through an hour of line shuffling before I called work to inform them I needed the rest of the day off. When it was finally my turn, I discovered they were conducting COVID temperature checks. The woman before me was apparently running a slight fever and was sent home to book another appointment available sometime in the next year or so. I prayed harder than I've ever prayed that I wouldn't be subject to the same fate. When it was my turn, temperature woman pointed the laser gun to my forehead and I thought, *Just do it. Put an end to this misery*, but apparently, I was fever-less and given permission to enter. The police officer manning the door gave me a skeptical up-and-down before I swung the thing open, thinking, *What's your fuckin' problem?*

Inside, I was instructed by another woman to apply enough hand sanitizer to wash a boat before directing me to stand in the back of yet another line. Hand-san lady asked what my business was there, which I explained. However, when that was the extent of our discourse and there was only one line to stand in any way I wondered if this was part of her job or if she was just being nosey.

After another thirty minutes of line shuffling, I was finally called up to the booth by some grinch in glasses. Barely audible, muffled by a mask and the plexiglass barrier that COVID supposedly knows not to wander over, the grinch said grinchily, "Can I help you?"

No, I just stood in line all morning to say hello…

"Why, yes!" I told her with a big fake smile. "I've just moved here, so I need a new license and to register my car, please."

In the early days of my DMV adventures, I always failed to bring some necessary piece of documentation and could never complete the transaction in one go (because, well, who possibly gets it right on the first try?). I'd forget my birth certificate or some such thing, so while standing at the window, going through paperwork, I'd text my mother and have her send me a photo of that little notecard that proves I exist.

"Sir, we need the *original* copy," booth person would say. "This perfectly good photo being held up by your biological mother will never do. Why don't you schedule a follow-up appointment for sometime next decade and we'll try again."

"B-b-but—"

"Next!"

Or they'd ask for some obscure thing that wasn't listed on the website. "And we'll need six proofs of address, an expired ID, your passport, a utility bill, a hand-written letter from your grandmother, your latest paystub so we know exactly how much money you make, and your middle school library card."

"B-b-but," I'd plead, "both my grandmothers are dead!"

"How about a pint of blood, sir? Did you bring your pint of blood?"

"Look, I'd be more than happy to slit my wrists right here," I'd say. "Do you have a Yeti tumbler or maybe a wastebasket to collect it?"

These days, I just bring every scrap of paper and hard drive I own that might contain a snippet of personal information. I dump an armful of crap on the counter asking, "Am I real *now*?" And so that's what I did here.

The grinch began sorting through my papers, throwing things back at me one at a time. "We don't accept Amazon packages as proof of residency here," she said with a disappointed sigh. "This W-2 is too old. This paystub doesn't have your full social security number." I began biting my nails as the pile of potentials got smaller and smaller. I was about to begin cutting my wrists with one of the rejection slips when she turned to the computer and began typing.

After a lot of vigorous clicking, she told me, "Stand on the X in front of the screen and look directly into the camera." After they suck the life out of you for two hours, they ask you to smile.

Not that it matters because no matter how hard you try, they still print that mugshot of some look-alike zombie in your place.

The credit card scanner beeped in front of me and told me $80.00 was due.

"Eight bucks?" I said as I plugged my card in. "Really?"

"Are your contacts in, sir?"

"I can see what it says just fine. I'm just wondering if the license is made of gold."

"Your contacts, sir," she said with thinning patience. "It says here you wear contacts."

"Yes, yes, they're in. Why?"

"If you have no further questions, please proceed to booth eighteen for your vision test."

"Okay, okay," I said, turning to move along. Before I left, I asked, "Do I need these utility bills anymore?"

"No, sir. Now please make room for the next person in line."

"Alright, thank yo—"

"Next!"

I began shredding any disposable papers and threw the scraps in a trash next to booth eighteen.

Booth eighteen man said, "Please look into the vision device and tell me what you see."

I stared into the new age equivalent of the E chart on the wall and rattled off a few letters.

"Very good, sir. It appears you're not blind after all. That'll be forty million dollars."

"Forty dollars!?" I said. "For a two-second vision test?"

"Sir, here in great the state of Calnnectassorido, we require you to be able to *see* in order to drive. There's absolutely nothing we can do."

"Nobody's arguing *that*," I said. "But I went to the optometrist last week and he charged me less. Do you at least take insuran—"

"Cash or credit, sir?"

"Credit," I sighed, plugging my card into the reader.

"Please go to booth thirteen to collect your license and register your vehicle."

"Alright, thank y—"

"Next!"

Grinch number two was a librarian-looking dinosaur who hated me and every other person who'd ever walked the earth.

Why do you people do this job? I wondered. *I can't believe the term 'Going Postal' wasn't applied to you assholes first.*

"Hi there!" I said happily. Librarian lady said nothing, just took my forms and began typing.

"Do you have a copy of your current lease?" she asked.

"Yeah, sure," I said, shuffling through whatever I hadn't thrown away. "Why?"

"I need to confirm your address."

"We just went through this rigmarole at the first booth," I said. "Why are we doing it again?"

"Standard protocol," she sighed with her ever-lasting hatred.

I wondered if I'd be paying for a second eye exam as well when she said, "Sir, it appears someone wrote over the last number of the original date where your lease ends."

"Yeah, I know," I said. "My landlord made a mistake and corrected herself. So?"

"Well, sir, this is a problem in the eyes of the great state of Calnnectassorido. This document appears to be tampered with."

"*Tampered* with? You're kidding me."

"No, sir. You see, it looks like your lease began as of July 2020 and ends in June 2020, but then someone wrote over it to make it read June of 2021."

"Like I said, my landlord made a mistake and corrected herself."

"Sir, I just can't accept this the way it is."

"The woman at the first booth accepted it the way it i—" I cut myself off to jump to another train of thought. "What are you even saying? That my lease is going to end back in time?"

"Sir, if you've got an issue, you can take it up with the state."

"The state? How about you call over your manager."

She rolled her eyes but did so.

A man younger than me came over and asked what the problem was. The dinosaur roared the situation at manager man and manager man said, "Sir, do you have any other proof of address?"

"I sure do," I told him. "It's right over there in that trashcan by booth eighteen."

"Terribly sorry about that, sir," he said staring at me, waiting.

"Are you…" I stared back, "expecting me to dig it out?"

"Sir, please understan—"

"Do you know *why* it's in the trashcan? Because after I went through all this shit the first time around at that booth over there," I said, shooting a finger in the general direction, "she told me I wouldn't need it anymore. And now you'd like me to dig through the trash for you?"

"Well, sir, I wouldn't *like* for you to dig through the trash, but without it…" he trailed off, shrugging as if to say, "What can I do?"

"Are you fucking kidding me right now? You really want me to dig through the trash in front of all these people after we've already gone through this process just so you can do it again?"

Manager man said nothing, just stood there looking as though he felt enough shame for the both of us.

"Fine!" I stormed over to the trashcan and plunged my hand inside and grabbed a handful of scraps. I stormed back over and slapped them onto the counter and said, "There ya go! Good luck piecing them back together, 'cause I'm not doing it."

He stared at my rubbish long and hard. "Well, um," he mumbled. "Perhaps, well, perhaps you have an image of something on your phone that shows your current address? I'd be willing to make an exception this one time."

"Are you shitting me right now? You had me reach my hand into the trash and now you're afraid to touch it yourself?" I pulled out my phone and started swiping through my emails with my grubby fingers. "You're a real piece of work, you know that?"

All he said was, "Do you want me to throw this away for you, sir?"

No, I'd like to keep it as a souvenir.

"I think it's the least you can do."

After that was settled (again), librarian woman said, "That'll be four-ninety-nine."

"*Five hundred* dollars!?"

"Four-ninety-*nine*," she corrected me, as if that one dollar made the rape consensual.

"The registration fee is *five hundred* dollars here?"

"Sir, in the great state of Calnnectassorido, this includes the Registration Fee, the Administration Fee, the Standard Issues Base Plate fee, the Title fee, the Safety Plate fee…"

The what..?

"…the Clean Air Act Fee, the Greenhouse Reduction Fee, the Passport to Parks Fee, the Age of Vehicle Add-on fee, the Emissions Area Air Account Fee…"

The who now..?

"…the Motorist Insurance Database Fee, the Road Safety Surcharge, the Peace Officer Standardized Training Fee…"

Peace Officer Trai..? Is that the parking guy outside?

"…the Specific Ownership Tax fee, the Prior Specific Ownership Ta—"

"Alright, alright, alright, I get it!"

"Sir, will that be cash or will you be taking out a second mortgage on your home?"

"Hold on," I said, "lemme sell a few stocks and drain my 401k."

I left the DMV that day with two new license plates, feeling a combination of murderous rage and elation that only comes from leaving such a hellhole.

In the parking lot, I discovered that whoever installed the license plates for the guy I purchased the vehicle from had stripped the plastic threading on the front plate holster. This meant that when I went to unscrew the old plates, the screwdriver just twirled aimlessly. I had to rip the plate off by force, ripping the screws out with it, then walk to a nearby hardware store to buy thicker ones. After that, I screwed on the new plates by cranking threads into the holster myself. Only after I got the front one fastened did I look down and realize the DMV had given me two mismatched plates.

"Just my luck!" I screamed. "Just. My. Fucking. Luck."

I unscrewed the new plate, screwed the old one back on, and marched right up the stairs ready to kick down the door and throw them at the librarian. Cop man saw me coming up the stairs and stepped in my way. He put a hand up to stop me and said, "Where do you think you're going?"

I showed him the plates and said, "They gave me the wrong plates. I need new ones," and started to walk around him.

He stepped in my way again and said, "I don't give a fuck, pal. You wait in line like everybody else." Then he jerked his thumb toward the line that still wrapped around the building.

"You listen to me, you power-hungry, take-my-job-too-seriously piece of shit," I wanted to say. "You don't even work here! You're just some Silverback Gorilla they hired to stand here between donut breaks!" But I did not say that. All I said was, "You're kidding me..."

He was not. He put his hand on his mace and took a step closer. Never have I wanted to slice somebody's throat with an erroneously registered piece of metal more than I did in that moment, but I backed away, steam rising from my ears, I'm sure.

There was another DMV about ten minutes away, so I figured I had nothing to lose by checking the line there rather than wait another hour or more here. I prayed there wasn't some prick holding a gun at that door, and there wasn't. I spoke to the young woman with the clipboard and explained the situation about the mismatched plates, and she let me cut right up to the booth.

The same librarian-looking creature sat at this one, like some evil twin in a parallel universe. She snarled at me, asking why I was jumping the line. I explained the whole situation, including the cop.

"So you're telling me you drove all the way up here from that DMV to try and swap those plates here?"

"Yes, ma'am. It's an injustice, I know. Now if you could jus—"

"Well I'm sorry, sweetie, but you can drive yourself right back down there because we can't help you with that."

"And why not?" I asked, face turning purple no doubt.

"Because those are *their* plates," she said. "*They* have to fix that for you."

"What does it matter? Plates are plat—"

"Next!"

By the time I got back to the first DMV, the cop was on break or off duty, so I marched up to the unguarded door and nearly ripped it off the hinges. Temperature lady pulled her gun on me, but then, softly, she said, "What are you doing back here?" All I did was show her the two plates, and she said, "Come with me," and walked me right up to the booth that'd fucked me over in the first place. "Seems like we gave him two different plates," temperature woman said to librarian-dinosaur one. "Can we straighten this out?"

"Oh, sorry about that, sweetie," said librarisaurus. "Gimme a second."

She turned around and shuffled through an assortment of presumably matching plates as temperature woman patted me on the shoulder and walked away. The librarisaur looked me up in the system again and made an adjustment, then handed me two *matching* plates this time. They began with the letters—and this is no joke—CRY. I almost did just that as I left the building that day.

I walked past the cop on my way out, back with donut crumbs on his shirt, of course, but I did not stick my tongue out as I walked by him like I wanted to, nor did I plant my ripped-out screws under his tires because I knew my own tax dollars would be repairing them. Instead, I screwed on the new plates as hard as I'd been screwed over that day and drove home.

All this to tell you that the next time I moved, I bought custom plates that read:

JSTMYLCK

ON RUNNING

"Everyone has a plan
until they get punched in the face."
—Mike Tyson

Do you ever see those people shadowboxing at the gym?

Who are they fighting? I wonder.

They could easily practice those moves at home or in a more appropriate setting, yet they choose to put their prowess on display at LA Fitness.

I joined a martial arts gym myself once. "Learning a martial art," they told me, "will fill you with confidence!" And they were right. After earning my first stripe as a white belt, I began to feel high and mighty. I walked around with my shoulders back further, my chest puffed higher, and I—*I*—was a tough guy now.

Soon after that milestone, I went to visit the great city of Nashville, Tennessee, where I ventured out to the bar scene alone one evening. I saw some live music, made some new friends, and had a generally wonderful time. I was feeling fulfilled and happy when fatigue rolled in around 3:30 that morning. That's when I decided to walk back to my car in a nearby parking lot.

Approaching a crosswalk at the intersection of two main roads, I waited for the sign to change to that little man giving me the okay. It wasn't busy at that hour. In fact, the only other person around was the woman standing beside me, crying. I wondered what she was sobbing for, but only briefly as I decided it was none of my business.

Suddenly, a black Escalade ripped up to the sidewalk and screeched to a halt before me. As the vehicle parked, the passenger door swung open, revealing another woman, also crying. I looked back and forth from this new woman to the one beside me and nearly asked, "Do you two know each other?"

But that's when a voice appeared from my left—a man's voice, a very angry voice.

That voice said, "Are you the one fuckin' with *my* wife!?"

This sparked confusion. If by "fuckin' with your wife" you mean standing here minding my own business, waiting to go home and reminisce on the lovely evening I've had so far, well then yes, guilty as charged!

I only had a moment to form the inkling suspicion that this was a case of mistaken identity. That's when the first woman shot a wide-eyed glance behind me and screamed, "*NO!*" This piercing shriek tickled my right ear at about the same time something tickled my left. Something firm. Something fast. Something fist-like, it turned out.

In the split second between her shriek and his impact, time slowed down. I'm not sure what I would have done to deescalate the situation, but I'd like to imagine myself addressing the owner of that fist in one of two ways.

"Why hello there, my dear fellow," I might've said in a calm, cool, and collected tone. "Have you considered taking heed of your wife's reaction to this ill-intentioned fist you're throwing toward my face? While I'm sure you have a perfectly sound reason to assault the perpetrator of your accusation, the man you're searching for is not, in fact, me."

With this, the man would freeze, his furious demeanor melt away, and he would lower his fist with a chortle. "Well then my apologies, good sir!" he would say. "*That* was a close one." Then he'd extend his hand, and we'd shake on the whole misunderstanding with a laugh.

In alternative fantasy number two, I would summon the powers of my newly acquired white belt and pull off a *Matrix*-like maneuver, spinning around to take the assaulter's back. From there, I would gracefully subdue him into a headlock, performing a citizen's arrest. I've known of the citizen's arrest for quite some time and had always dreamed of pulling it off. Here was the perfect opportunity.

Unfortunately, I had no time to perform either of those things because I was too busy stumbling about as the world began to ring. In the direction of which my head had recently been spun—to my right and downward—I saw, through a twinkling of stars, the hat that formerly sat atop my head now lying in the street.

That's weird, I thought in the manner in which cartoons address Tweety Birds. *How did you get down there?*

Then I raised a hand to touch my burning ear and felt the warm liquid that was now trickling down my jaw. When I realized it was red, my brain snapped out of that spangly daze, and my body flooded with adrenaline. I turned to see what had caused this recent infliction of pain.

It was not the sophisticated gentlemen with whom I'd clarified the misunderstanding, nor was it the scrawny aggressor whom I'd placed under citizen's arrest. No, through my blurring vision, I looked up to see that fist attached to a shirtless man in designer jeans, guido in nature, and inflamed by what I can only assume was a cocktail of steroids and cocaine. His eyes were crazed with fiery rage, and veins pulsed on his temples. And around his neck, dangling from a chain, was Jesus.

As the man cocked back his arm to rain down more blows, I learned a few things. I learned that in real life, "martial" "arts" are not a choice. I learned that when caught off guard by a psychopath who'd have no qualms about killing you in a public street, a primal survival instinct kicks in. I learned that under these circumstances, "I" was no longer in the driver's seat. When the time came to make one of three decisions—engage in rational dialogue, perform a citizen's arrest, or run the fuck away—my body chose for me. And so, I ran like one might with a murderous Italian maniac chasing behind them.

After a block or so, I sensed this faithful Christian had given up on me, so I slowed down to collect my wits. *Well that was exciting!* I thought, head now throbbing in pain. But in all that excitement, I had left my hat behind. I really liked that hat, plus my vehicle was in the opposite direction anyway, so I chose to return to the scene. My hopes were that this man had lived out his delusion of rescuing his wife from evil ol' me, and that he and his princess had ridden off into the sunset in their Escalade. This, however, was not the case.

As I crept up the sidewalk down which I'd just been chased, I found the man and the woman standing in the middle of the street, screaming at each other. If we're being honest, I felt honored that she'd come to my defense that way. She even went so far as to slap him across *his* face.

This, he did not care for—not one bit. And in the same manner in which he had plowed his fist through my ear, her mouth got the same treatment.

She dropped—*hard*—to the pavement. Her purse went flying and belongings scattered. Like a gentleman, though, he picked them up for her. Then he helped her to her feet by nearly ripping her arm out of its socket and escorted her to the Cadillac firmly. He opened the door and tossed her in the back seat along with her things and slammed it behind them. I made brief eye contact with the second woman, who was understandably more hysterical than before, as the man hopped in the driver's seat and sped off into the night. I caught a final glimpse of the tears streaming down her face as the door closed and I bent into the street to claim my hat.

Later that night, I lay in bed, replaying the situation over and over in my mind. I wondered what had gone wrong in that man's life. I wondered what the real perpetrator of that accusation was doing as my head throbbed in pain. I wondered about the fate of those two young women. But mostly, as I drifted off to sleep that evening—exactly as you're not supposed to with a concussion—I wondered how many hours of shadowboxing in the gym it would take to prepare for such a thing. Then I figured, *Maybe I'll just take up running*.

COACHING

*"Whenever I see a woman with a bratty kid I think,
I hope that orgasm was worth it!"*
—*Unknown*

In my late twenties, I took up a job coaching youth soccer in Boston. When I say "youth," I mean sometimes as young as kindergarten. For anyone who hasn't looked up the origins of that word, let me enlighten you.

"Kindergarten" is of German descent, derived from two root words: "kinder," meaning children, and "garten," meaning garden. A man by the name of Friedrich Froebel combined the two to create the literal meaning, "a garden of children."

"The discoverer of the method of nature," as he so pretentiously deemed himself, compared his method of developing intelligence in children to the way a master gardener studies the individual natures of plants. This, of course, is done by placing them in circumstances and atmospheres which enable them to grow, flower, and bring forth fruit.

I don't know if Froebel has actually met any Kindergarteners, but if by "grow, flower, and bring forth fruit" he meant "cry, terrorize, and tell shitty jokes," well then he was dead on.

"Knock knock!" the four-year-old begins.

"Who's there?" you play along.

"Me!" replies the child, excitement building in their eyes.

"Me who?" you reply.

Then, panic. "Uh... Um..." they stumble as an awkward tension builds and confidence drains from their face. "Uh... C-c-can I start over?"

Sure kid. Wipe that snot off your face and do what you gotta do.

Half of these kids were always covered in boogers. Not one of my first graders, though. He devised a system that made sure his face was always booger free. You see, mucous never had a chance to drip down past his nose because, well, his finger was always scooping it into his mouth so frequently. This quick and repetitious motion was executed with the smoothness of machine, performed with more desperation than Pooh Bear reaching for the dregs of honey in his jar. A man who stumbled upon a water fountain in a desert wouldn't satisfy his thirst so quickly. If this kid put half as much effort into playing soccer as he did eating his own boogers, we'd have a regular Lionel Messi on our hands.

Don't get me wrong: working with kids is rewarding, but they are truly disgusting creatures. Sometimes, our practice fields were right next to playgrounds, where kids would jump in and out of the public litter box and run up to give you a hug. My favorite was when you didn't catch sight of a sandy, three-foot-tall human running head first into your crotch. They'd collide with full impact, latching onto you with those grubby little fingers as their hands began to wander toward uninviting places. I wanted to tell those little dick-grabbin' perverts to cut that shit out, but it's not their fault my privates were at eye level for these reverse pedophiles.

Even when they make it past the earlier grades, things didn't seem to get much better. Every child these days can navigate the world of gaming to learn the *Fortnite* dance, but few can seem to tie their own shoes.

For those of you out of the *Fornite* loop, it's a multiplayer shooter-survival game that involves battling underworldly creatures by building defensive fortifications. If it sounds complicated, just know that all the characters have one thing in common: their fucking shoes are tied. You'd think if we're preparing our future generations for the zombie apocalypse, we'd at least cover the basics.

"So, what are you learning in school?" I asked a fourth grader while tying her laces.

"Geometry," she replied.

I was stunned. "You're learning the branch of mathematics concerned with the properties and relations of points, lines, surfaces, solids, and higher dimensional analogs, but you don't know, 'Over, under, around and through, take Mr. Bunny, and pull him through'..?"

"No," she giggled.

Do you know the last time I used geometry? Fourth grade.

Do you know the last time I tied my shoes? Four hours ago.

What are we doing in our school systems, honestly?

In full disclosure, I had to Google that rhyme—as I, for one, am fully capable of tying my own shoes without the aid of bunnies—and along with it, I'd like to point out, came a list called "Shoe Tying Tips for Parents."

The list began, "If your child gets frustrated, take a few-week break," and I immediately threw my computer in the trash.

A few *weeks*!? Your child has only been *alive* for a few weeks. Your child's attention span is a few seconds at best. Just point behind them and say, "Look over there!" Then back to their shoes and say, "Oh no! Your shoes are untied!" It's practically an eternity in their eyes.

The list went on: "Velcro is still a cool option."

No, it's not. Your child has Instagram and has yet to see anyone on the Red Carpet wearing Velcro. Besides, by the time they're joining recreational sports leagues and learning the rules of complex games, they should be able to wrap their pretty little heads around tying a simple knot.

"Straddle the child while tying their shoes," the list continued, "so they can see from your point of view."

Just make sure it's your own child you're straddling or you'll belong in jail from a jury's point of view.

"Practice tying something bigger, like a jump rope around a tree!"

Or a noose around your neck to save yourself the trouble.

It's a well-known fact that the first thing NCAA basketball coaching legend John Wooden taught his players was how to properly tie their shoes. It's a lesser-known fact that the only reason he wasted his time on such trivial bullshit was that parents let their kids get all the way to college, tripping over their own two feet.

Parents, do your fucking job. In addition to lacing up their shoes, please teach your kids basic principles of how to succeed in life so that I don't have to. For instance, while coaching, I had a very low tolerance for poor sportsmanship. I'll give you an example of what I mean.

We used to play a game called Star Wars. The object of the game was to be the last man standing. The players, representing

Jedi Knights, would all line up on one side of a giant coned-off rectangle. When the coaches, or evil Sith, yelled "Go!", all the kids tried to run across the field without being tagged by a soccer ball below the knee. If a player was tagged, they were to grab a ball and join the coaches on the sidelines as the Dark Side.

While explaining the rules of this game, one of my first graders heard "Dark Side" and pointed to my black assistant, yelling, "I get it! Cause you're dark!" If there were a striking system in my book, this would have been all three.

I lined those kids up, and when I yelled "Go!" who do you think I was aiming for? I let that little bastard get just far enough to think he'd gotten away with what he'd said, then—*Boom!*—fired off a laser and tagged him right in the ankle so he tripped and fell before the finish line. He hit the ground—*hard*—and justice had been served. [Blows off blaster and returns to holster.] Or so I thought, because he bounced right back up and scooted across the line to safety as if he'd never been tagged.

*A racist **and** a liar?* I thought. *Not on my turf.* But I gave him one more chance, just for dramatic effect.

This time, as soon as he stepped off the line—*Boom!*—ankle, ground, tears immediately, justice served. Or so I thought, because that kid popped right back up again. This time, though, he marched straight over to one of the other coaches, about forty years his senior, and pointed a furious finger at his face. "You stop this game *right now!*" he screamed, tears streaming down his cheeks.

That coach bent down and firmly explained how children are not allowed to speak to adults that way. Secondly, he added, rules are rules and fair is fair. That kid kicked and screamed and cried and refused to join the Dark Side. I was appalled when that coach caved so easily and gave the kid another chance as long as he promised to play by the rules from now on. The kid agreed.

Now, if you think I'm above beaming the same five-year-old three times in a row with a soccer ball, you've got another thing coming. We lined them up, and when I gave the word—*Boom!*—ankle, face plant, tears. But this time, the boy bounced off the ground stumbling and screaming to his daddy like a little bitch.

That may be your daddy back home, I thought, *but **I'm** your daddy in this galaxy!*

[Cue "Imperial March": *Duh- Duh- Duh- Dun- DunDa-Dun- DunDa- Duh-*]

I maintained a straight face on the outside, but on the inside, I keeled over with laughter. I may have booked my first-class ticket on a plane crashing in hell, but in that moment, burning for eternity seemed worth it to teach that little fucker a lesson. And don't you judge me; someone had to, 'cause he sure as hell ain't gettin' them at home.

Anyone who's worked with large groups of children for more than a few hours can sympathize with this one. Any teacher, camp counselor, or coach knows there are times when some kids deserve a good slap upside the head. Not all children! And not all the time. But once in a while, there's a gremlin who needs to be taken down a notch.

I once coached a session with a middle schooler who would not shut the fuck up when I was talking, wouldn't abide by the rules, and wouldn't even sit out of practice when I tried to punish him. That kid was a real piece of shit, and I never wanted to punch somebody in the face so badly in my life. Even the other boys his age gave him looks like he was being an asshole, and that's saying something. But realistically, what could I do? Lay a finger on a child and you lose your job in today's world. I'd never felt so powerless as I had when that little brat wreaked havoc on my entire session, and all I could do was think, *Your parents did a real bang-up job raising you, ya mutant!*

After practice, I followed him to the parking lot, determined to speak to his mother. But when I saw the permanent look of remorse glued to that woman's face for bringing her own child into this world, I couldn't bring myself to make her life any worse. I had spent one hour with this devil; she was committed to a lifetime.

I think a big error in our progressive ways is neglecting to leave a bit of leeway when it comes to child abuse. I don't mean dishing out unnecessary punishment, or taking it too far, or allowing asshole parents to abuse their power; I'm simply envisioning a world where if a parent came to pick up a child from practice, and that kid cried about the coach giving him one good smack, the parent would just assume they deserved it like they did in days of old. No formal complaints, no lawsuits, just take the kid's TV away and help the lesson sink in. Is that so much to ask? Or have I just been flagged by child protective services?

The softness with which we pamper children these days is doing more harm than good. Take, for example, this everybody-gets-a-trophy mentality.

You come in first? You get a trophy.

You come in last? You get a trophy.

You quit halfway and never finish? Trophy for you, too.

What lessons are we aiming to instill here? To incentivize those who give up to receive the same as those who work hard to succeed? We may as well punish the hard workers instead. In the end, we're accomplishing the same thing.

What happens when little Billy, who received a trophy for everything he's done whether he was good or not, goes off into the real world and discovers his upbringing was a lie; when his safe little bubble is burst and his false sense of self-esteem is no longer there to protect him; when he learns that professors and employers and the IRS don't give a fuck about his cabinet full of participation trophies; when he becomes an adolescent who never learned to deal with disappointment and failure and heartbreak and rejection now has to deal with them for the first time, previously pumped full of belief that he could just participate (or not) and everything would be daisies. Well, what happens is that for the first time in his life—and far, far too late—Billy crumbles, unprepared by those who thought they were doing him a favor.

But I digress…

Actually, no I don't. Don't raise a Billy.

Anyway, Star Wars.

After the game, that older coach came up to me, his eyes oozing the weariness of a man who drinks his career choice away. With his usual stone expression, and in his deep Welsh accent, he said to me, "I noticed you went right for him again." Unable to tell whether or not this was an accusation, I said nothing in return, only stared back with a stoic gaze of my own. There was a long moment of tension between us, but as he turned away, I caught a smile flicker across his face as he said, "Good." At least somebody understands.

When I worked with kids, I could see their future; when I dealt with parents, I could see their past. As we grow up, some things change, but many stay the same. The social dynamics learned by children often dictate how they interact with the world as adults. For what is society but one big playground?

I coached a pretty young third grader named Brooke once. Even at that age, Brooke knew she was pretty. She'd absorbed it from her mother, who had the habit of flipping long blonde curls over the shoulder in a pompous manner displayed by both parties.

It seemed Brooke already knew how the juxtaposition of having a less skinny, less pretty friend would accentuate her beauty. I think this is the only reason she convinced Ali, her clumsier, chubbier sidekick, to accompany her that first day.

In the case of sports, though, it was Ali who was excited to be there, to learn about soccer for the first time. Brooke just sat, pouting, undoubtedly dragged there by her mother, who needed someone to live out her own childhood dreams. But as the days of practice unfolded, it turned out to be Brooke who discovered she had the natural ability and was praised by the coaches for a job well done. Ali, meanwhile, struggled and became frustrated that in this aspect of life, too, it was Brooke who was winning.

By the third grade, Ali already knew she would never get the same attention as her pretty friend did, but she stuck by her side anyway. Better to have the popular girl on your team, was the unconscious rationale, because perhaps you can collect the overflow of attention if there was any. But envy brews at a young age, so when the praise wasn't administered in the doses Ali desired, she reverted to temper tantrums and tears to draw more attention her way. With an encouraging but neutral tone, I explained that if she wanted to get better, sitting down in the middle of the field and stamping her feet wasn't the solution. I told her to keep a level head about herself and that, with practice, she would improve. She wasn't very accepting of my advice, as it wasn't what she was looking for, so I left her alone to mull over what I had told her.

Moments later, though, another coach approached to console her in the manner you would a baby—"What's wrong, sweetie?"—reinforcing her behavior.

What's wrong is that life isn't fair and my parents made me ugly, I articulated in my mind what Ali would later discover for herself. Then, continuing with the narrative which would remain the unconscious story of her life, *so if I kick and scream people will pay attention to me!*

At soccer practice we took water breaks as a group, 1) for the sake of time and efficiency, and 2) to encourage team behavior. Brooke knew this, but decided she was thirsty and shouldn't have to wait for everyone else.

"Can't I get water *now*?" she asked me.

"There's only a few minutes before break," I told her. "You can make it."

"*Pleeease*," she begged, batting her eyelashes at me.

"I think you'll survive," I said with a wink, denying her charm as gently as I could.

She folded her arms and stormed away, then immediately approached one of the other assistants to perform the same routine. He, though, fell for the eyelashes and granted her permission, unraveling the subtle lesson I was trying to provide.

Brooke used her premature beauty to get her way, Ali adopted a crummy attitude to get hers, and the world catered to both of their impulses while I felt alone in trying to teach them lessons they could use.

But then again, who was I to play God? Brooke will likely grow up and, like her mother before her, find friends and men who cater to the whims doled out by batting eyelashes and flipping curls, while Ali will seek out those who fold in the face of temper tantrums and stamping feet.

Had I been doing my part to show these kids that the world doesn't always give you what you want for being pretty, annoying, cheating, or not being able to tie your own shoes? Or was I simply imposing my own ideals on the way I wanted the world to be? I don't know; maybe everyone *should* get a trophy. But maybe, at least for now, that's why I've hung up my whistle on coaching.

DENTISTRY

[Jerry Seinfeld]: I am not an anti-dentite!
[Cosmo Kramer]: You're a rabid anti-dentite! Oh, it starts
with a few jokes and some slurs: "Hey, denty!" Next thing you
know, you'll be saying they should have their own schools!
—Seinfeld, Season 8, Episode 19

"What do you mean it's stuck!?"

This is what I garbled as the dentist's fingers became trapped in my mouth. But let me explain how we got there first.

Like anyone with an ounce of common sense, I was convinced the dentist is a scam. I mean, they used to fill people's mouths with mercury and asbestos or whatever. These "doctors" take advantage of the poor souls who feel brushing their teeth on occasion won't cut it. I, on the other hand, was wise enough to avoid this semi-annual money pit from the age of eighteen to twenty-eight, at which point I finally got a job with insurance and decided to see what all the fuss was about.

"Do you come to the dentist often?" the nurse asked from behind her mask.

"Ohhh, once every decade or so," I laughed nervously, as she strapped on her gloves.

"I see..." she replied, failing to hide a tinge of concern. "Well, let's take a peek then, shall we?" She scanned her assortment of torture devices and picked one. "Let me know if this is sensitive," she told me, stabbing a sharp claw into my gums.

"Uh-huh," I tried to say. She furrowed her brow, surprised that probing a fishhook into someone's mouth would inspire sensitivity.

She dug and pulled at various toothy surfaces before she removed her hands and asked, "Did you have braces?"

"No," I told her. "Why?"

"You have very nice teeth."

"Oh, stop it," I said, loosely flapping a wrist in her direction. "I bet you say that to all your patients, don't you?" She laughed, so I feigned a blush and said, "Not bad for ten years of neglect, huh?"

"Oh no," she replied. "You've got a *ton* of buildup in there." She swapped her tool for a more daunting one as she told me to open wide. I did. She said, "This might tingle." It did.

I imagine the merciless scraping of ten years' worth of crud from under your gums "tingles" about as much as getting tattooed under your fingernails. Occasionally, I'd catch a small pause in the torture where I spit out something like, "I think I taste blood." She'd promptly gun me down with that water pistol before scraping onward with another scythe-like object.

"I don't recall the dentist hurting this much as a kid," I told her during another break in the action.

"Gets worse as you age," she told me, gouging into an exceptionally sensitive crevice. "After ten years," she assured me, "today will be the worst of it."

After today, I thought, *I'll see you in another ten years.*

This process went on until I was bleeding from every tooth and gum, at which point she called over the doctor for a second round.

"It's not as bad as you might think," the doctor told me, jabbing her hooks into my toothy hole.

"Really?" I asked when she pulled her hands away. "Because it feels pretty bad."

"Do you floss?" she asked, wrapping what appeared to be some rope the size of a bungee cord around her fingers. She didn't wait for an answer, just leaned over, struggled to force it between my teeth, and leveraged her weight when they wouldn't give way. Eventually, with a *pop!*, she sliced into my gums.

I planned on telling her I use flossers the next time she stopped to wash the blood away, emphasizing something like, "With *floss*, not three-ply twine," but I never had the chance.

"Uh oh," she announced, struggling to remove her hands from my face. "It's stuck."

"Wha oo ou ean i's uck!?"

There were some unyielding yanks to and fro before the nurse had to get involved, holding me down as the two of them jerked me around.

"I'm having a hard time getting in there," the doctor said after the nurse cut her loose. This was said in a condescending tone, as if I should have been born with bigger gaps between my teeth, as if the spatial layout of my jaw was something within my control, as if *I* was to blame for *her* inconvenience.

"I fucking noticed," I said, or at least I wanted to.

"We'll have to do a deep scaling," she announced, removing her gloves in a manner that expressed she'd given up on me. "Can you come back next week?"

"Excuse me? A what when?"

"It's a deeper cleaning," she explained. "How are you with needles?"

"In my mouth? Huge fan. Why?"

"Novocaine," she said coldly.

"But the nurse told me today would be the worst of it!"

"You'll *hardly* feel it," she scolded me like a whining child. "We'll drill these cavities the same day."

"Caviti—" I fell short as the more appalling word sank in: "*Drill!?*"

It seemed that going to the dentist more than once every decade wasn't a conspiracy after all. In fact, some might even classify it as a "good idea." But when I returned a week later for the follow-up, I had apparently adopted some mutant ability to heal. I no longer required the deep scaling, and, in addition, one of my cavities had magically disappeared.

"I can't even seem to find the other one!" the nurse told me.

That's because it never existed, you fucking shyster, I thought but did not say.

The remaining cavity was—allegedly—just a small depression on the surface that didn't require the power drill I had imagined. Instead, she used a small spinning file that required no numbing agents whatsoever. I was out of there in ten minutes with a patch job I could have botched myself with some spackle from Walgreens. At least that would have saved me the considerable fee for the second visit my insurance didn't cover for me. It seemed they could have easily done that procedure the week prior, but they always find a way to getcha, don't they?

THE PHLEBOTOMIST

Phlebotomist, defined by the Cambridge Dictionary:
a person who is trained to draw blood from a patient

Phlebotomist, defined by Urban Dictionary:
a real-life vampire

"Ohh," she sighed at my query of how she landed in such a field, "I've wanted to be a phlebotomist for as long as I can remember."

Is that... normal? I wondered, staring up as the woman hovered over me, fumbling with a blood bag. I thought most little girls longed for occupations such as Actress, Teacher, or Veterinarian. But no; while the other girls were role-playing movies or healing stuffed animals at recess, this one wanted to puncture veins. I was about to probe further as she gazed off in reverie through her glasses, but she continued on her own.

"I've always had a thing for blood," she confessed, now attaching the needle that would soon collect mine. "I love thriller novels and murder mysteries. Have you seen *Hannibal*?"

I had, but all I could think was how while my parents were reading *Good Night Moon* as a bedtime story, hers must've thought *Dracula* to be a suitable choice. I'm ashamed to admit I didn't even know the term "phlebotomist" before looking it up prior to this encounter, meanwhile this little munchkin knew she'd be bloodletting from the time she could hold a decent conversation.

I observed her more closely as she coddled my limp arm, pressing around the pit of my elbow with her thumb. I didn't care for the way she kept squinting, as if her prescription was a tad outdated.

"You have very nice veins," she told me with a smile. "I don't even need to use the arm band!"

Is that... normal? I wondered. I mean, if I were trained in the art of withdrawing another's most vital resource—which, admittedly, I'm not—I would like to think I'd at least follow protocol no matter how much my ego insisted otherwise. But no; here she took a deep breath—summoning her inner Hannibal Lecter, I presume—and focused her attention. She paused to recite some kind of internal dialogue, perhaps a cult-like prayer, just before she plunged the needle so deep that I felt a startling pain shoot down my arm.

"There," she exhaled, satisfied as the tube ran red. "Now you just relax."

Stomach clenched, arm throbbing, I gave the back of her head a stiff nod as she left to tend to the other victims. It amazed me how many of us volunteered to be there, spilling blood like livestock on a vampire farm.

So time slowed, as it does when nothing's happening. A countless spell drifted by as I stared into the rafters of the local high school gymnasium. I watched new people come, and others go, and it seemed like I was there for quite some time. At some point, I turned to peek at the tube of red dangling off the table and out of sight. There was no way of knowing just how much blood had been drawn by that time; it could have been an ounce, it could have been a pint, or, for all I knew, they could have taken it all.

As I wondered what was taking so long, it was as if a second phlebotomist read my mind. She approached with her head slightly cocked to the side and peered below the table with a questioning look upon her face.

"Are you feeling okay..?" she asked—something I'm sure everyone finds comforting while being phlebotomized.

"I think so," I told her, now questioning my own well-being. "Why?"

Phlebotomist #2 traced her line of sight up the tube and toward the needle that was plugged into my arm. "Seems like it's taking a while," she said. Then, with a raised fist of demonstration, she added, "Would you mind pumping your hand?" I complied, though I felt this was only slightly more courteous than a quick zap with a cattle prod.

"Should my arm, you know, hurt?" I asked as a sharp pang pulsed with every flexion of the arm.

She dismissed that by saying, "No, that shouldn't be the case," as if I'd asked if it's dangerous to draw blood on Wednesdays.

I looked up and caught the eye of Phlebotomist #1 off in the distance, blindly stabbing another needle into another arm or some such thing. She seemed agitated, concerned, maybe even hurt. When Phlebotomist #2 left my side, after doubling down encouragement for the old pumping routine, #1 shuffled over, wearing a look of self-conscious disdain as she examined the contents of my bag.

"What was she saying?" #1 snipped in a hushed voice.

"Umm, apparently, it's taking a while and I should pump my hand to speed up the process."

"Well *I* could have told you *that*," she declared in a snooty tone. Then she shot a dirty glance over at Phlebotomist #2.

I began to ask if my arm should hurt like this, but before I could finish, she was gone. So there I lay, altruism painfully squirting from my vein with each squeeze.

There was a rumor of snacks after the whole ordeal was over, so that's the carrot I focused on as the needle tickled my flesh. The woman who interviewed me about the condition of my blood—inquiring about any shared use of drug needles, whether or not I've ever paid for sex, or any chance I may have unknowingly contracted AIDS—had mentioned juice boxes and pretzels. This excited me because, well, I don't think I'd sipped from a juice box since before I knew what AIDS was!

I was daydreaming of these snacks when Phlebotomist #2 walked by and noticed my fist pumping had slowed to an undesirable pace. "Keep going!" she sang, flexing in rapid demonstration as she passed.

I pumped out the last few drops over the course of the next few minutes when finally Phlebotomist #1 informed me that my duty had been fulfilled. I was relieved to have the needle removed from my arm and bid farewell to the bag of dark liquid that was once inside me.

After being bandaged and sent to the recovery table, I found there were, indeed, juice boxes and pretzels, along with cookies and fruit gummies to boot. And—a bit out of place, I thought— there were also salmon sandwiches. Now, I have nothing against mashing up fish and mayonnaise to be spread on bread the way you might tuna, but how long should those things be sitting at room temperature in a high school gymnasium? It's not like there was a line out the deli door and these things were being restocked by a fresh supply. No, these perishable gut traps had been parked on that table for who knows how long, enduring who knows what degree of spoilage, surely sickening whatever poor souls were sucker enough to try them. Not me, though. Mm-mmm. I wasn't falling for that old "Swap a pint of blood for spoiled goods" trick. No, I crammed down my fair share of *non*perishables, even pocketed a few for the road, then got the hell out of there.

Right before I slipped out the exit door, though, Miss "What are the chances you have AIDS" handed me a pamphlet. On it was aftercare instructions, a hotline to call if complications occurred, and a date in the near future which she pointed to repeatedly, telling me would be the next blood drive.

"I thought you could only give blood every—"

"Fifty-three days," she finished my sentence for me. And it was with a used car salesman's smile that she added, "We've planned accordingly."

These were clearly the smartest vampires I'd ever encountered, and I wanted nothing more than to leave. I booked it all the way home, sat down to eat some leftovers before bed, and proceeded to unwrap the bandage on my arm. No sooner had my bottom hit the chair than I popped right back up again when I saw a half-golf ball-sized knob had grown under my skin. I left my dinner behind and drove back to the vampires' layer, burst through the door, and asked, "Is this... normal?"

Failing to restrain a look of subtle alarm, Miss AIDS shuffled me over to a seat and fetched an ice pack, assuring me that everything was just fine. Phlebotomist #2 sauntered over to see what was the matter and appeared to shake her head disapprovingly at the scene. Phlebotomist #1 caught wind of all the commotion and burst through the growing circle of phlebotomi, nearly elbowing over #2, with whom at this point it was clear had some sort of phleboto-rivalry going on. That's when she lifted the ice bag to witness the result of her botched phlebotomization.

"Ohhh, it's not so bad!" she hissed in a you-big-baby tone, eyes rolling at the lump that was now really only missing a Nike swoosh. With that, she forked over the ice pack and merely walked away. She didn't even offer the apologetic glance one might expect after having their vein mispunctured by someone who spent their childhood dreaming of puncturing veins.

In the end, it was at least two weeks before the painful throbbing subsided. The woman on the other end of the "Call if you have concerns" hotline assured me that my entire arm turning a rainbow of purple, green, yellow, and blue was a healthy sign of recovery. She guessed that the needle may—*may*—have traveled a smidge deeper than necessary and might have struck a nerve. I was to avoid lifting heavy objects or doing anything strenuous for at least a week, and just before she hung up the phone, using that rapid disclaimer voice they play at the end of infomercials, she slipped in that if things got worse, I should head to a hospital immediately if not sooner.

"You know," Miss AIDS had told me shortly after I walked in the gym that day. "You really are doing a good thing here, and we would love to see you come back again and again." It was then she added, in a slightly confused tone, "Statistically, most people never return after donating the first time."

And it was here that I thought, *I can't imagine why…*

FIVE TIMES

If God had intended us not to masturbate,
He would have made our arms shorter.
—George Carlin

So, how many times in one day have *you* masturbated?

"When I was your age, I jerked off five times a day!"

These were the words my boss once bragged to me.

At eighteen, I worked in the construction industry—one of those crude and unpolished environments every teenager should be exposed to. One day, my boss dropped this line during a conversation, to which I said, *"Five* times!? You're an animal!"

"I'm *Italian*," he smugly replied, as if having genes of that origin could explain how ejaculating a fifth time wouldn't expel a piece of your soul. I descend from European regions only a few borders away, but never did I strive to enter The Fivers Club at that age.

I don't know about your masturbatory habits—perhaps they involve candles and Barry Manilow, or a rose-petaled bath, or maybe you just duck into a storage closet on your break at work—but whatever they involve, it comes with some commitment of time. I imagine setting aside five chunks of time per day to squabble with your genitals adds up rather quickly. That time could be put toward—oh, I don't know—learning an

138

instrument, or spending time with your dying grandmother, or finding a cure for cancer. *Anything* that involves becoming a more productive member of society.

After one time, I'm about ready to get on with life. The desire to masturbate doesn't usually nag me again until sometime the next day or so. Maybe—*maybe*—if I'm feeling ambitious, I'll crank out a second round before bed that evening. But five?

Then there is a certain amount of chafing that comes with this level of masturbation. Regardless of how much lubrication is used, there is still a degree of friction being created. How long was he rubbing himself each time, you ask? Who knows. It could be five minutes, it could have been fifty, but let's drop the average somewhere in the middle and say between fifteen and twenty. Try rubbing any other part of your body—an elbow, for example—for a vigorous ninety minutes day in and day out, and tell me there's not a degree of irritation.

Also to be factored into the equation is the decreasing level of sensitivity. In the first round, you're like a virgin, thinking of clouds in the sky so as not to release too quickly. In round two, you're like Superman, feeling you can go all night long. By the fifth round, I imagine you're so numb you could start a fire like you're rubbing sticks together with that level of friction. It's just not healthy.

Regardless of knowing this back then, hearing about his accomplishments inspired me to push my limits to three. But as it turned out, I am not Italian. This was a bit much for my ancestral lineage, and tearing my frenulum was a lesson learned the hard way.

For those of you who don't know what a "frenulum" is (pronounced | ˈfrenyələm |), it's defined as "a small fold or ridge of tissue that supports or checks the motion of the part to which it is attached." It's that little thingy under your tongue that keeps it from falling back into your throat while you sleep so you don't choke and die. This example used in this definition, however, fails to mention the frenulum uncircumcised men have attaching their foreskin to the head of their, well, you know, penis.

When I say "tear," I don't mean there was a geyser of blood erupting from my crotch or anything, but rather a small, micro-tear that would only be visible to those who got up close and personal. The point is that my poor frenulum would never be the same. It would heal for a while, then tear every so often—say, in the clutches of a partner who yanked on my dick like the only source of water in a desert they'd been crossing.

Years went by before I found a job with decent insurance, at which point I stubbornly admitted to myself I should probably seek out a urologist. That, of course, wasn't before I did some research into what may be the solution for this type of injury.

Through a Google search, I found out that a "short frenulum" was not uncommon amongst foreskinned men such as myself. I even learned that it could, in fact, lead to the kind of blood-spouting injuries that mine, fortunately, did not. I came across the term "frenuloplasty," an outpatient procedure that involved surgically detaching the foreskin from the head of the penis by making an incision along the frenulum, then stitching the wound back together.

A few months prior, I had considered Lasik surgery. I descended into the YouTube rabbit hole and watched some gut-wrenching procedures that involved slicing off someone's cornea before peeling it away. I had trouble enough stomaching those, but, foolish as I am, I was drawn to the search bar once more like a moth to a flame. It was awful. If you're squeamish,

I would not watch frenuloplasty videos before bed unless you enjoy nightmares. However, I am going to describe one here because, well, if I had to suffer through learning about penis surgery, then you should too.

Without any kind of *You must be 18 years or older to watch this video* warning, I was thrust into the view of a man's flaccid penis poking through surgical attire, narrated by a man with an accent so heavy he butchered the English language as painfully as he described butchering his patients' genitals. (Just for the record, I would like to state that I'm not penis-phobic, per se. Sure, in gym locker rooms, for example, I tend to shy away from glancing at the numerous wrinkly cock-and-balls flaunted by old men—all too proudly and comfortably, I might add—regardless of how nice or ugly they are. And I think we all know, deep down, what I mean when I say "nice" or "ugly." Everyone who has seen more than one porno in their lifetime has a collection of reference points on the spectrum of dicks this world has to offer. I think we're all on roughly the same page when we see a young lady penetrated and think either, *Hmm. She'll probably enjoy that,* or, *Yikes! What is **that**!?*) Seeing the mutilation of a nice penis would have been scarring enough, but to watch an ugly penis get chopped into a more derelict state made things worse. Just to paint the proper picture, on a scale of "I mean, if I were gay…" to "*Christ,* that's an ugly dick!" this YouTube penis was clearly the latter.

I was about to exit the screen before I saw any more when something happened where I could no longer look away. That is to say, a giant needle entered the screen and stabbed this poor man's cock on its underbelly.

I think you know what I mean when I say I couldn't look away. It's that old train-wreck-in-slow-motion reflex, or the scary movie with hands over your eyes, but you peek anyway. You don't *want* to see what happens next, but the reality is you can't help yourself.

What happened next was that the thumb on that syringe pressed downward until a gumdrop-sized bubble inflated under the skin of that man's shaft. Here, I wanted to puke. The syringe was removed from view, but the bubble was not. That same thumb re-entered the screen and then pressed down upon it, vigorously shaking back and forth to disperse whatever local anesthetic had been injected. In that moment, I felt my own dick go numb at the very idea that this may soon happen to *me!*

Sure enough, a week later, I was sitting in a frigid room at the urologist's office.

"So why are you here?" the doctor asked me on the day of my examination. I suppose I should have been thinking about an answer to that inevitable question, but all I could think about was how they *knew* I had to pull my pants down in front of this stranger, yet cooled the room to shrinkage temperature.

"Would it have killed you to put a space heater in here?" I wanted to ask. "God knows you're billing my insurance enough to afford one."

Also, for some reason, I had it in my mind that the doctor was going to be a woman. Nothing against male doctors, it's just that I typically find women more comforting in the face of uncomfortable situations. When an older gentleman walked in, I'd be lying if I said I didn't feel a pang of disappointment. *But then again*, I thought, *maybe he can relate. Maybe he can offer some compassionate understanding for my dilemma.*

This, however, turned out not to be the case. He burst through the door in that hurried manner doctors do and, without so much as an introduction, asked, "So why are you here?" This was said in a tone that suggested I'd cut into his lunch break.

"Well," I began, averting my eyes from his gaze. "I, uh, well, I tore my frenulum." As I looked away, I caught sight of an enormous bottle of lube staring back at me from the counter. A pair of rubber gloves lay next to it and one of them appeared to be pointing at me.

In the manner in which he might ask his wife why she bought three salad spinners from Walmart he said, "Why would you do that?"

There was an awkward pause where I didn't know what to say.

"Why don't you get undressed," he added, "and let's take a look." Then he turned to give me a fleeting sense of privacy as he strapped on his gloves.

"By 'undressed,'" I wanted to ask, "do you mean completely?" But I didn't because the very thought of asking that question made me feel stupid for some reason.

My pants had to come off; that part was obvious. But what about my shirt? Was it also necessary? If I didn't take off my shirt, I'd be standing in a room with another man wearing a shirt but no pants. Is that less awkward than standing in a room with a fully dressed man while completely naked? And what if I take off my shirt, but when he turned back around to find me completely naked, a look of confused judgment scrunched upon his face as to why I was, in fact, completely naked? Then there was the matter of my socks. Do those stay? What combination of socks and shirt or no socks and no shirt would make things worse? These were the kinds of questions running through my mind as I felt very small, scared, and alone in the world, and the clock was ticking.

Eventually, I decided to recline on the doctor's table, as the sound of that crinkly paper gave me even more anxiety, fully dressed with my pants pulled down enough to reveal my, well, injury. This seemed an appropriate choice as the doctor turned back around, and his face remained expressionless—bored, really. As he stood over me, his stoic face made me long for a female doctor even more. Not only was I about to feel the tension one man might when another man closely inspects his heterosexual groin, but I was about to do so for someone who appeared to hate his job, who seemed to be having a bad day, who hadn't a care for the vulnerability his patient was feeling at this time. But it was too late for feelings.

I was hoping I could just show him the injury myself, but no, he insisted on getting involved. And unless I've blacked out any previous encounters, this was the first man to ever really touch me, you know, down there. In my youth, my family doctor had made brief, annual examinations just to make sure everything was okay, but I don't recall him making any notable physical contact. This frenulum inspection was by far the most intimate I'd ever been with another man. Both of his hands were used to roll my shaft from one side to the other repeatedly, in concert with pulling foreskin to and fro. He leaned his face close to my nether regions for a better look as he created this friction as I laid there, tense as could be, praying there were no... unexpected movements. No sudden increase in blood flow. No late-life realizations.

I have nothing against homosexuals; it's just not a surprise I wanted sneaking up on me this late in the game. It wouldn't have been the end of the world, I suppose, just a wrench thrown into the whole life plan. I'd already gone through a long and winding journey exploring my sexuality with women; to discover I'd also have to go through that same journey with men seemed like a massive inconvenience. Not to mention it would come at a time when my dick was out of commission.

There were none of those, though. And as I pulled up my pants, the doctor explained they'd have to perform a minor surgery, just as I suspected.

"I'll put you in contact with the surgical scheduler," he told me as he opened the door to leave.

"Well, wait," I stopped him. He paused, still holding the door open, and looked back to sigh as if I'd just ruined his day. His reaction left me feeling pressed for time, so I nervously fired off every question I could think of.

"Well, when do I need the surgery?"

"And how long will it take?"

"And how long is recovery?"

I imagine any rational person would have expected their doctor to close the door and resume the conversation in private, but this one did no such thing. A nurse walked by within arm's reach as he told me, "We'll slice up your penis as soon as possible." Maybe he didn't say it quite like that, but he may as well have. "The procedure takes about thirty minutes," he went on. Meanwhile, I stared out at the office staff, shuffling about their daily duties of faxing copies and whatnot. I suppose I shouldn't have felt embarrassed, as these strangers do work in urology after all, likely dealing with this sort of prognosis every day, but it felt like a matter of principle that any discussion regarding my privates should remain, well, private. Not with this doctor, though. With the door wide open for all to hear, the man described how a scalpel would be used to cut away the thin banjo string that now attached my foreskin to the head of my shaft. "Then," he explained, "they'll stitch you back up with an enormous needle, and recovery takes three to six weeks."

He turned to leave, and I hopped off the table to follow him, hammering him with more questions. He stopped, gazed absently toward me like a stray dog who'd followed him home and sighed, "The surgical scheduler will call you. She'll provide you everything you need." And with that, I was dismissed.

The surgical scheduler did not call me. After a few days waiting in silent expectation, I called her. She ran me through a number of questions that began with things like, "In the event you were to need a blood transfusion," as well as instructions like, "You'll be sedated, so make sure you have a ride home."

Imagining the endless scenarios in which my penis may spurt so much blood that I would need a transfusion was one thing, but the embarrassment of finding someone to drive me home from surgery due to vigorous masturbation? That was another.

"So…" I imagined stalling for time as I answered my prospect's question of what the surgery was for. "How many times have *you* masturbated in one day?"

I thought of the needle plunging into the YouTube penis to administer a local anesthetic. In that moment, it seemed less painful to find another doctor to perform the surgery in that manner than to find a ride after being sedated.

When the surgical scheduler informed me of who would be performing the procedure, and that coverage by my insurance would only begin after I'd filled my $3,000 deductible, I decided to search elsewhere. That is to say, I chose not to pay Mr. Warm and Fuzzy Sunshine there the three grand out of pocket to slice my cock open with a knife. Instead, I found another doctor who could perform the procedure with the local anesthetic, sparing me half the cost and the full embarrassment of finding a ride home.

A week later, when this second doctor burst into the room and failed to look me in the eye or introduce himself as well, I discovered Urology is not a field pursued by empathetic types.

"So what are we doing today?" he asked with the emotional capacity of a large rock.

I laughed at his joke, already lying on his table with my pants down awaiting his procedure. Then he stared at me, wondering what I was laughing at, and held eye contact with an expectant gaze. I cleared my throat. "Um, frenuloplasty?"

"Ah, okay," he said, enlightened to the purpose of our meeting now, fumbling through something on the counter while I wondered what I'd gotten myself into. I stared off into the ceiling, far enough above my head where I hoped I could avoid seeing whatever it was he'd turn around with. It wasn't far enough. Out of the corner of my eye, I caught a glimpse of the largest syringe I'd ever seen in my life. It was a needle Bugs Bunny might use if he were playing a doctor on a Saturday morning cartoon. In this moment, every fiber of my being clenched, and I closed my eyes and refused to open them again until this man had left the room. What I felt, though, was him lean into me, grip my penis in one hand, and then stab it seven or eight times in various places with the other.

There was no, "Are you ready?" or even a, "You might feel a slight pinch." Nothing; just *stab, stab, stab, stab.*

Who's a big brave boy!? I told myself the way a mother might a child. *Yes you are. You're a big brave boy!*

After he finished, the doctor asked, "Did that hurt?"

Tensed the way one might be after a stranger went to town on their most sensitive appendage with a needle, I squeaked out a big brave lie through held breath: "Nope. Not a bit!" I'm not sure what hurt more: having my cock stabbed by a giant needle or feeling the need to lie about it to the stranger who'd stabbed me.

"Good," he said, standing upright and disposing of the syringe. "That was the worst of it." Here, I let out a sigh of relief. That is until he added, mostly to himself, "So to speak." At this, my mind raced through the numerous interpretations of what that little phrase might mean. Before deciding upon any of them, I was alone.

"My name's Kyle, by the way," I said to the empty room.

Spanish music flowed from a speaker overhead and filled the silence. I'm not sure what the lyrics were saying, but part of me thought it was better that way. I closed my eyes and tried to drift into relaxation the best I could as my penis went numb, still exposed to the open air.

My eyes popped open again two songs later as a woman entered the room without knocking. Refusing to look in my direction, she began putting on gloves as she told me, "I'm here to clean you."

"Nice to meet you, Heretocleanyou," I did not say. "I'm Kyle. Would you like my consent before you touch my privates, or don't I have a say in the matter?"

I refused to look her in the face as she approached my exposed genitals in fear of any kind of reaction she might unconsciously let slide. Good or bad, I didn't care to know what this woman thought of… me.

How many dicks has she silently judged in her day? I wondered.

As she grabbed mine and wiped it down, she announced, "Alexa, play Lana Del Ray." Apparently, the Latin vibe wasn't cutting it in terms of mood music for wiping my balls with disinfectant solution. Instead, we were serenaded with the song "You're Pretty When You Cry," which turned out to be a more fitting tune considering what was about to go down.

After wiping to her satisfaction, the nurse grabbed a package off the counter and opened the kind of pad you'd see in a cardiac defibrillator. She unraveled a long wire and plugged it into some machine mounted on the wall overhead. Then she peeled off a sheet to expose the sticky part of the pad and asked me to lift my hips so she could stick it to one of my butt cheeks. After doing so, she turned for the door without explanation and grabbed the handle.

"Um," I meekly stopped her in her tracks. "What's that for exactly?"

She stopped, looked at me with boredom, and sighed, "It's a grounding wire." When my eyes widened in both shock and confusion, she said, "So you don't feel the electricity." There was a tense pause while she searched my face for a sign that this answer had alleviated my concern. When she found none, she added, "To stop the bleeding?" Then she turned and left without bothering to search my face for anything more.

A short while later, the doctor barged in again with another assistant in tow, no eye contact from either.

"Are you numb?"

At this point, I figured that the lack of eye contact was best for everyone.

"I think so?"

That was good enough for him. He instructed the assistant to "Hold him." She took a tentative look at my frightened penis, glanced back up at the doctor with an expression I interpreted as being her first day on the job, then walked over to stand beside me.

The doctor fumbled through a collection of clanging metal tools that made my gums tingle while the assistant complied. I'd been emotionally numb during sexual encounters of my past, but being physically unable to feel the touch of a woman down there was a first.

The doctor turned and got to work as I spent the next twenty minutes with my eyes closed, pretending what was happening wasn't happening. Mostly, I tried tuning into Lana's voice, but when the machine overhead beeped and the onset of a crackling noise ensued, I was scared back into the present. I didn't dare look at whatever "the electricity" was, but I did experience another sensation.

Ah, I remember thinking, *so that's what burning penis smells like.*

After the doctor sewed me up and told me it was all over, I opened my eyes and thanked the man who spends his Saturdays sculpting penises like mine. Then I hoped never to see him or any of his nameless assistants ever again.

When I remained in the office waiting room about five minutes longer than advised, Miss "Hold him" approached me with a smile. I smiled back, prepared to respond that I was doing fine, thank you for asking, when she said something in the warmest tone anyone had addressed me all day: "You can leave now."

On my drive home, I wondered how many mutilated penises I would have to see before becoming as cold and dead inside as people who work in urology. I found my answer when I got home and unwrapped the dressing to see my dick for the first time: One.

I *freaked* out at the sight of the bloody, burnt, stitched, swollen, discolored, and disfigured appendage that was now dangling between my legs. In that moment, I wasn't sure I'd ever be able to look myself in the eyes again, let alone another human being. I collapsed into a hysterical fit of laughter and prayed this was all a bad dream.

What had I done in a past life to deserve this nightmare? In a flash, I'd never felt more alone in my life, because who do you call to talk through the emotional backflip caused by the sight of your surgically mangled penis. The stoic doctor? The nameless nurses? Your mommy?

There was nothing in the recovery packet beyond, "Wait twenty-four hours before washing your penis with soap and water." Anything would have helped to acknowledge those initial feelings, even something as simple as, "Refrain from jumping off a rooftop based on the assumption your sex life is over." I mean *anything*.

As I stood there, hyperventilating and laughing myself onto the verge of tears, I decided there are some things in this world that a man just needs to get through on his own. I calmed myself down and looked into the mirror and became the doctor I needed me to be in that moment. Not so much the "Who's a big brave boy!?" type of doctor, but rather one who offers a rational hand on the shoulder and an explanation that this how things initially look after surgery, that this is a temporary experience, and that everything is going to be just fine.

This took more than a few tries as "patient" me kept slipping back into emotional outbursts while "doctor" me had to continue comforting him. We got through it eventually, though. Pulling up my pants to employ the old "out of sight, out of mind" routine worked wonders for us. I had to keep telling myself this would all make for a good story one day.

As the last of the numbing agents wore off, I waddled upstairs as if I'd just ridden a horse across the Sahara Desert and back without a saddle. There, I climbed into bed and put on the movie *Training Day* to distract myself from the pain. And it worked… right up until Eva Mendes came on screen.

THE GROUCHY PIGEON

*"These pigeons
have been living with each other
for ten or fifteen years,
but when I throw feed down,
they kill each other to get it."*
—Mike Tyson

A "grouch" is defined as a habitually grumpy person. Sulky, complaining, and morose are also words found in various sources.

That's me. Sullen, ill-humored, irritable, all of it.

Have you seen *Gran Torino,* with Clint Eastwood rocking on his porch as a cranky old man? That's what I'm like on the inside, at thirty-one I might add.

I don't know how this happened. One day, I came across a mug that said, "Sometimes I stay inside because it's just too peopley out there" and I thought, *I could drink coffee and Bailey's from that mug on a porch in the woods for the rest of my life and be satisfied.*

Planning to stop by for a visit? I would have cleaned up, but I wasn't expecting company between now and death.

I recently moved to Florida—because that's what old and cranky people *do*—the Sunshine State known for white sands and bikinis. I rent a lakeside condo and, instead of staying out late to party by the beach somewhere, I find joy in rising early to watch the ducks and pigeons from my balcony. Every sunrise. Wouldn't miss it. I have no idea how I became this man.

To be fair, the pigeons—or "mourning doves" as I call them with a pinky raised in the air—really are a sight to see. They've got that whole hive mind thing going on, where when one decides to do something, all the rest jump on board. When one is hungry, they all gather in a flock and start pecking at whatever crumbs, seeds, or garbage is around. In the air, their collective noun changes to a "flight" of pigeons, where if one veers right, they all veer right, soaring in circles, silhouettes with the backdrop of the rising sun in the background. I find this mysterious and wildly entertaining in my apparent old age. It makes the start of each day a little less grumpy.

What are some fun pigeon facts, you ask? Why, I'll tell you.

Wikipedia will inform you that 20-70 *million* of these game birds are shot annually. But don't you worry your pretty little head: couples raise up to six broods of two young—or "squabs"—every year. This means there's basically an infinite supply, so… eat up!

Did you know pigeons are monogamous? I guess the song that mentions two turtle doves was on to something. Listen to Wikipedia's description of their mating practice—conveniently abbreviated with brackets and ellipses for comical effect by yours truly—and tell me it doesn't sound like someone you know:

The male will approach the female with a puffed-out breast, bobbing head, and loud calls. [...] The male then leads the female to potential nest sites, and the female will choose one. [...] The male will fly about, gather material, and bring it to her

[...] then builds it into the nest. [...] Mourning doves will sometimes requisition the unused nests of other mourning doves, birds, or arboreal mammals such as squirrels.

You see what I mean? The parallels between pigeons and people are uncanny. I can see why Mike Tyson took a liking to these birds. In fact, I feel like I'm becoming more and more like Mike Tyson by the day: angry, bitter, chip on the shoulder, future heavyweight champion of the world. The only true difference between us that I see is that I own a George Foreman grill and I imagine he does not. Oh, and the tigers. My condo has pet restrictions.

So, I don't know about *your* ducks, but whatever breed they've got paddling around the questionable Florida waters of *my* lake sound like velociraptors. To me, this confirms the theory that birds evolved from dinosaurs. I mean, everything else in Florida resembles creatures from another time—alligators, pythons, iguanas, Donald Trump—so I'm keen to throw ducks in that category as well.

If you'd see these ducks, you'd know what I'm talking about. They're more aggressive than your average quacker where I'm from up north. I don't know if it's the biohazardous sewage they're dining from, or something they're fed every night by the lonely woman who visits them below my balcony.

I suppose you're wondering how I know she's lonely, and it's just a hunch, but what gives it away is how she knows every duck by name. You heard me: she's *named* the ducks.

"Good evening, Gerald! How are we today?" [tosses a steroid-infused crumb]

"Looking handsome as usual, Harrison!" [flicks a Hulk snack in his direction]

"There's plenty to go around, Tommy! That wasn't very nice…" [wags a finger]

I don't know if she's confused or projecting an ideal reality, but to her, all the ducks are male. Or maybe she's just selective in who she feeds. Or perhaps she thinks all ducks are male. Or, for all I know, she had a bad experience with a female duck at an impressionable age, as I did hear her tell Tommy that if he put his beak on her one more time, she would promptly kick him in the face. Look, I'm not here to judge lonely people—and who knows, with her duck fetish and my pigeon infatuation, we could make the couple of the year—but what I'm getting at here is that I've done the neighborly thing by *not* telling her to get the fuck off my lawn.

I could easily be *that* guy. You know the one I mean: the self-proclaimed wildlife expert, patrolling the local parks to scold any father-daughter combo criminal enough to carry bread without a license.

"You really shouldn't feed the wildlife," they say. "It interferes with their natural dietary selectio—"

Oh, stop it. That's what ducks are for.

We've all met this guy in some form or another. Maybe he's that know-it-all at the grocery store who offers unsolicited advice in line as you ogle the last-minute snacks.

"Don't do it!" they advise. "That's how they get ya!"

"Listen, *buddy*. I think I know what is and isn't good for me," I say as I slap a candy bar on the conveyor belt as an impulse buy.

These are all the same breed of people—ones who got told what to do in childhood, so they take their frustrations out on the world as the opinion police, violating anyone within earshot with their thoughts and ideals.

That mug was right as far as I can tell: It *is* getting a bit too peopley out there.

We weren't meant to live like this—stacked on top of each other, domesticated, and pretending to be polite to every stranger to cross our path. Honestly, are most of these Joes and Janes actually contributing anything to society? Or are they just consumers, pushing the 1-click button on Amazon to receive more crap on their doorstep tomorrow?

Most people just seem to be in the way, you know? I mean traffic? I'm over it, aren't you? And it's not the rush hour traffic I'm upset about—that's understandable. It's the three in the afternoon on a Wednesday traffic that gets me going.

"Who *are* all you people!?" I scream through the windshield. "Are we *all* blowing off work to get to the bank on time?"

Where could a million people be off to on a weekday afternoon? Don't they have *jobs*?

Remember the pandemic? When everyone was afraid to leave their homes for a while? Those were the days: a time when a good public health scare cleared the highways for miles at a time. Was it too much to ask for a brief zombie apocalypse to cull the herd?

Look at the great TP shortage of 2020. People were fighting tooth and claw to get the last roll off the shelf. Mike Tyson meant it literally when he said, "These pigeons have been living with each other for ten or fifteen years, but when I throw feed down, they kill each other to get it," but here it paints a beautiful metaphor.

Let me ask you something: Do you know the difference between a pigeon and a dove?

Me either. All I know is that when I hear the word "dove," I picture something beautiful and elegant, free to flutter about the sky. "Pigeon," on the other hand, is abrasive to the ear. Listen to it: pidge-in. Not to mention you can't spell the word without "P-i-g". It brings to mind some feral creature that shits on the statues that represent better times.

I know this, yet I can't shake the more pessimistic analogy to suit the human race. We'd rather kill each other over scraps of tissue to wipe our ass than embrace the bidet. That's who we've become.

Not me, though. I'll be that pigeon that soars left when everyone else turns right, the one that hunts for seeds when everyone else fights over crumbs left by the woman at the pond. That's me: the rogue bird on the fringe of bird-ciety, balking at the flock, or flight, or whatever the cool birds call the masses these days. You can find me in woods, rocking on the porch, embracing my newfound spirit animal: the grouchy pigeon.

COLON CLEANSE

"You aren't what you eat,
you are what you don't poop."
—*Wavy Gravy*

"Pissin' out the ass" is an official term my doctor friend once used. It wasn't until I performed a "Saltwater Flush"—the consumption of two-and-a-half teaspoons of salt in twenty-four ounces of water—that I truly understood the meaning.

Let me take a step back, though. It wasn't until the second time I got COVID that I was inspired to cleanse my colon. Although a milder case this time, I'd been getting sick more than usual over the past few years and thought a serious detox might help my immune system. I could have gone to a reputable healthcare blog, or the YouTube channel of someone with a medical degree, or, you know, consult my own doctor, but naturally I began with the search bar on Amazon. When the first review on the first product had more than sixteen *thousand* thumbs up for a title that read, "I found God in a grocery store bathroom stall," I figured I was on to something.

This reviewer explained that the reason he was in a grocery store in the first place was because after starting this colon cleanse, he'd burned through five rolls of toilet paper in three days and needed to re-up his supply. By the time he'd reached the store, his tummy was rumbling with gas again and he felt "a full-on avalanche approaching." He quickly shuffled into the store in search of a restroom and described himself walking like The Hunchback of Notre-Dame by the time he reached the base of the stairs up which the bathroom was hidden.

He made the mistake of trying to relieve some pressure by squeaking out a bit of gas on his way up. "That wasn't gas," he described, realizing his mistake was enough to "break the dam of fecal hell."

Here's what happened next:

At this point, I had nothing to lose and sprinted into a stall. As I sat there, an absolute mess in a graffiti-ridden grocery store bathroom, I started reflecting on my life's choices, and what led up to this moment of utter embarrassment. It was at that moment that I found God. I sat there, not quite in tears, praying for a change of lifestyle, asking God for forgiveness of my sins. I started thinking of the dog I gave away when I couldn't responsibly take care of him, the girlfriend I cheated on in college, and other life-long regrets. After about twenty minutes, and another round of colon discharge, I got myself together only to run out of toilet paper again. (My sincere apologies to the Kroger store in Virginia, as I had to use hand towels to clean up, clogged the toilet, and left my underwear in the trash.) My last mistake, which was technically my first mistake, was wearing grey sweat pants and not wearing a baseball cap to hide my shame.

Other reviewers chimed in with things like, "It's 4am and I'm currently in the bathroom with diarrhea as severe as I had on a trip to Pakistan."

Another said, "I'M MELTING OUT MY BUTT. Please save me!!"

And yet another: "I Didn't Find God In a Bathroom Stall, but this stuff is THE BOMB. And by the bomb, I'm referring to whatever I've been dropping in the toilet since taking this. My poor dog hides under the bed anytime I go to the bathroom now. Oh, a piece of advice: Never trust a fart."

For $17.99, I thought, *this sounds like the cleanse for me!* And I'm no math whizz, but as long as I was going to be quarantined near a toilet for the next week, a seven-day cleanse shipped overnight to my doorstep just seemed to add up.

Below is a log of my week-long journey. That is, if you have the stomach to bear what mine could not.

Day 1: The instructions said to begin with a single capsule, instead of the recommended double-dose, taken at night before bed. The next day I was shitting a purge of diabolical diarrhea in copious amounts like I'd never seen, all throughout the day. Most of it was orange and fibrous, a reflection of the fruit I'd had that morning, but others were shades of dark murk I imagine only exist in the Devil's den. The only short time I dared to be a sprint away from the toilet was to hit the drive-thru pharmacy at Walgreens for an affirming COVID test.

Day 2: A couple hours after I took another single dose and went to bed, I awoke to a painful bloating and dangerous motion in my guts. My eyes burst wide open as I threw back the sheets and made a sprint for the john. I got there just in time to unleash a gaseous explosion and dark spell of who knows what. It was awful. Evil really. Had I let loose in my sleep I would have had to burn the mattress and dump the ashes into a biohazardous waste bin.

Day 3: On Day 1, I had read about other ways to flush your system and came across the "Saltwater Flush". I trust it tastes like the seawater you might gulp down after being trounced by a wave on summer vacation. This concoction is chugged down with the intention of purging your body of excess waste and toxins by forcing a bowel movement through the imbalance of salt in your system. At least that's what I gathered from the red-headed man I found on YouTube with enough followers to at least *seem* credible. It wasn't until after I swallowed what could have been a dangerous amount of sodium that I considered confirming the claims of this internet ginger with an actual credible source.

Healthline.com told me that although there is no scientific research backing any of these claims, there was plenty of anecdotal evidence. I should be warned, however, that such a degree of electrolyte imbalance may lead to muscle spasms, weakness, confusion, irregular heartbeat, blood pressure problems, or seizures. But it was too late for that.

I thought tag teaming this cleanse might speed up the detox process, and boy was I right. What my doctor friend referred to as "pissin' out the ass" ensued no more than ten or so minutes after consuming this drink and plagued me for the next hour.

If you pumped a Super Soaker to the max and shot it straight into the toilet from an inch away, the echoing backsplash would be a fraction of what I was experiencing. At one point, I thought I might be launched from my seat like one of those water propulsion jet packs. I'm not positive a Salt Flush is what Adele was referring to when she set fire to the rain, but perhaps she also found God in a bathroom stall.

Keep in mind I was dealing with COVID as well, now blowing waste from my nose *and* my asshole simultaneously.

Why did I choose to detox at the same time I was sick you ask? Because I'm a fucking moron.

Any time I thought I might be done and got up to resume my day, my stomach would say, "Hey, remember me? Why don't you sit your ass back down." I complied every time. It wasn't worth the risk of painting my apartment the color of my insides. And sure enough, like Old Faithful, a geyser of liquid would spew from my rear.

What is happening!? I thought in blend of panic and curiosity. *How is this even possible?* At this point, my intestines were merely a Slip-and-Slide for whatever I'd poured inside them.

By the one-hour mark I had spent more time on the toilet than off that morning. I was beyond wondering how much could be left in there, as the water bottle I'd consumed must have already run through me in a salty, fecal stream three times over.

My final squirt was enough to fill a glass of water with as clear a liquid as I'd drank down in the first place. I'm not sure which ingredient of the laxative cocktail was to credit for this total evacuation, but I was sure glad it was over.

Day 4: Solid poops? Hah! Those were a thing of the past. My digestive system was now a leaky faucet on a hair trigger. Squatting down? Bending over? What were those like, I struggled to recall. Any wrong step could have led to sharting, any sudden movement to soiling myself, and I only dared wear underwear I'd have no problem never seeing again.

Why would I choose this as the day to introduce juicing and "toxin binders" to the equation? Because I'm an extremist, it would seem.

My bowels had been largely emptied and I was minimizing my food intake—due to both illness-limited appetite and for conscious cleansing purposes—so it seemed like an appropriate time.

The juicer I ordered arrived on my doorstep within a day, so I began with whatever was in my fridge (mostly apples and oranges). The benefits of consuming vitamin-rich drinks are obvious and well known, so I won't spend time rationalizing it here. But I also ordered a combination of calcium bentonite clay, activated bamboo charcoal, and psyllium husk powder. This warlock's brew is supposed to absorb toxins, heavy metals, and other harmful materials so you can excrete them from your system. I figured as long as I was excreting so much, I might as well draw out as much evil as I could.

Now, the existence of "Mucoid Plaque"—or some combination of harmful, mucous-y material and food residue that coats the gastrointestinal tract—is up for debate in the scientific community. Seemingly qualified professionals on both sides of the equation have differing opinions on whether or not this collection of sludge has been rotting in the crevices of your intestines at all. But the anecdotal evidence you see of people who are willing to share photos of their excrement is astonishing.

The images you, not-so-squeamish folks, will dare to witness by Googling "Mucoid Plaque" are, well—"unsightly" would be an understatement, and "gross" wouldn't do it justice, so let's just go with—thoroughly disgusting. Multi-foot-long strings of rubbery, tar-like substance are being excreted after performing this treatment. Oh, and apparently it smells like decaying fish that have been baking in a minivan on a hot summer's day.

Whether or not this is quackery, if I could potentially remove anything that smells like that from my body by consuming a few reasonably priced supplements that have other benefits on their own, I figured it was worth a try.

Day 5: The morning after the first double-dose was a novel experience. It brought me back to the time as a boy when I read that cute little children's book called *Everybody Poops*.

"Not like this they don't!" I yelled as I let loose a bubbly, moistened fart like you wouldn't believe. "No one prepared me to poop like *this*!"

I'm talking about a gaseous expulsion you wouldn't care to dream came from inside you. Rippling, curdling sounds that putrefied the air while I was held seated hostage by the same uneasy bowels that produced the aroma. If COVID were ever to take my sense of smell away, that would have been a convenient time. But no, there I sat, tortured by my own home-brewed sewage and filth.

Whatever war this double-dose waged while I was asleep felt like my innards were being scraped free of any lingering feces that might've clung to their walls, by a rake. Then a Zamboni began driving around to polish them clean. The cramping I woke up to in the wee hours of that morning lasted longer than the intermission of a hockey game, though. Let's just say it was dark when I shut the door behind me and daylight when I emerged.

My poor toilet, man. I felt like I should write it a poem or something, maybe buy it flowers. I've never been more grateful that it was working, more thankful for modern plumbing. I don't know who has to deal with this stuff after I'm done with it, but I sure am glad all I have to do is push a button and make it disappear. These weren't dumps I'd wish to leave in an outhouse somewhere, or even deposits I'd make in a porta potty. No, these deserved to be flushed out of existence, if not blasted into space.

This wasn't the blackened tar I was promised from the binders—that was a long-term play—but if I had to name the palette of modern art my bowels painted that morning, I would have gone with *50 Shades of Brown.*

*What kind of person **am** I!?* I thought as the shame seeped in. *Could **anyone** still love me if they knew of this?*

Not only would this display have been created by every tan, orange, and brown a jumbo box of crayons had to offer, but we're talking about a full spectrum of textures plopped out in various groupings as well.

The relief I felt as that masterful work of art swirled down the drain was both mental and physical. I felt lighter in more than ways than one: free, as if I'd shed baggage that had polluted me for a lifetime.

Day 6: I'm not going to say that things began to slow down by this point, but enough so that I decided to introduce suppositories into the equation as well. You know, for science. And because apparently, I'm a masochist.

In my research of detox methodologies, I came across this home-brewed concoction that involves melting organic cacao butter into slender ice cube molds, then adding a mix of antiparasitic essential oils to be frozen, and then shoved up your bum.

You'd be shocked at the images of what people have found lurking up there—from gross little parasites to full-grown tapeworms. They are truly and utterly repulsive, and I wanted none of them living inside of me if there were any.

And there were. First, the oils jostled loose what appeared to be ancient-looking turds wrapped in webbing, as if some intestinal spider had spun them like flies to suck whatever fecal nutrients might remain. Then, things. Creatures. Little intestinal critters of varying shapes, sizes, lengths, and colors that I had no idea were inside of me or for how long. Stuff you absolutely wouldn't believe was crawling around your intestines until you saw them come out for yourself.

I was shocked. I'd considered myself healthy. How could this be? Was I dreaming? No. Numerous unspeakable parasitic monsters dropped into the toilet one after another from inside of me. Who knows where they came from. Late-night fast-food extravaganzas from high school, perhaps, shoveling down Grade E "meat" you wouldn't even feed your dog. Or maybe from the tainted meals I'd consumed while abroad, where I'd contracted giardia, *twice*. Who the fuck knows. But there they were. And I sure was glad to be rid of them.

Day 7 or so: When the Mucoid Plaque came, boy, was that enlightening. The odor description, I'll agree, was spot on. *That was a part of me!* I thought. But no more. No fucking more. I went through an all-out war with by bowels that week, and I won. I. fucking. won.

Was it fun spending the first hour of every day glued to the toilet, you ask?

Was it worth enduring a new stomach cramp every morning?

Would you spend another week running to the toilet so often you'd wished you'd wore a Fitbit to count the number of miles you'd logged?

I'll answer these questions with another question: Will *you* walk through the valley of the shadow of death and fear no evil for God is with you?

As it says in Psalm 23 lines 1–6: "thy salt flush and thy suppositories, they comfort me."

I'd do it again in a heartbeat to purge those devils from my body. Getting COVID for a second time was the best thing that ever happened to me if this was the detox rabbit hole it sent me down. All the ungodly gurgling, all the satanic shitstorms, the preposterous poop-a-thons, the fantastical fecal matter, the eruptions, the explosions, the volcanos: it was all worth it. Though I spent a week of my life blowing mucous out of both my nose and my ass, to rid myself of all the evil I saw, being lightened the way I am now was more than worth the journey.

But if I can leave you with one piece of advice, dear reader, it is this: If you do plan a multi-method colon cleanse at the same time you've contracted Coronavirus for the second time, never—and I mean *never*—trust a fart.

FISHING WITH JOE

"See you later, alligator.
After a while, crocodile."
—Bill Haley

In hindsight, I may have done a stupid thing. Well, it was trusting, anyway, not necessarily stupid. At least it turned out that way. But if you had clicked on the news and seen my gnawed and mangled body floating in the Everglades with a headline that read, "Trusting idiot found raped and murdered," you would have thought it was stupid.

So, to back up a minute, I met this ex-military outdoors enthusiast at the archery range. I'm new to the range, so I stopped to ask him a question or two. We got to talking about outdoorsman's things, as outdoorsmen do, and one thing led to another, and we swapped numbers with the intention of shooting together to prepare for the upcoming hunting season.

A couple of days later I received a text that said, "Do you like fishing?"

I do.

A follow-up text said, "Do you know how to kayak?"

I do.

Another said, "Do you know how to swim?"

I do.

My new friend then called me to explain that he got off work early and planned to kayak into the Everglades for some of the best bass fishing I'd ever experience, if I wanted to join.

I did.

So, Joe, as we'll call him (chosen for the abbreviated version of G.I. Joe), came to pick me up in his pick-up truck about thirty minutes later with kayaks and gear.

Now, keep in mind these things that I neglected to at the time:

1) I'd only conversed with this man for total of one hour.

2) I have never ventured into the vast and shifting maze of unrecognizable landscape that is the Everglades.

3) The story I had that best painted a portrait of Joe's personality was a joyful tale of a hunting trip he'd gone on for a three-hundred pound hog. This beast was shot at and pinned to the ground by his ballsack, which lead to some wildly entertaining grunts and squeals, as Joe told it. Eventually, though, he plugged another arrow into the back of its skull to put an end to the ordeal.

On the drive over, Joe shared more stories. There was his deployment to Afghanistan with a colorful commentary about the people who live there, a description of China and Russia as inferior superpowers to the United States, theories of government-buried secrets regarding extraterrestrial technology and tax expenditure, and so on in similar veins. All these things were relayed as he spit the by-product of chewing tobacco out the window, and I was eating it all up. (The stories, not the chewing tobacco that is.)

When we got to the boat launch and put the kayaks in the water, the only other boater there was turning around to motor down the main channel. He asked us over the purr of his engine, "You guys ever have issues with gators in those things?"

"Gators?" I said, my voice cracking as I confirmed what I'd heard.

The man in the boat nodded toward the water about eight feet from where our kayaks were parked. Sure enough, gliding along the surface were the black and boney protrusions of what became apparent was an alligator's back.

"Ah," I gulped, clearing my throat to address him in a more manly tone. "Gators."

"Eh, I've never had much trouble," Joe said.

What do you consider "much"? I wondered, but I refrained from asking in fear of looking like a "pussy," as military personnel refer to frailer men.

Being a northerner, I had never seen a real-life alligator before. This particular specimen was no Godzilla, per se, but not an animal I'd want jumping onto these open-style kayaks to take a nip at my toes either. This creature appeared to pay us no mind, though, and kept moving down the channel as the motorboat man puttered in the opposite direction doing the same.

Joe pushed his kayak into the water and hopped in. I did a quick scan for any more prowling reptiles before doing the same. Instead of the main channel that ran along civilization and the safe banks of the mainland, Joe paddled across the river toward a narrower stream with a sign that read, NO BOATS BEYOND THIS POINT.

As if anticipating my question, he yelled back as we passed, "Too shallow for motors back here."

I nodded, then replied, "Just out of curiosity"—*not because I'm a pussy or anything*—"what's the biggest gator you've ever seen back here?"

Joe put his paddle down so he could hold up his hands about the distance apart that a baking sheet is long.

Oh, I thought. *That's not so big.*

Joe bobbed his hands up and down for emphasis before adding, "His head was this fuckin' wide. Must've been twelve feet long."

"Twelve feet!?" I said. "Are you shitting me?"

"Longer than your kayak," Joe said. "He was a fuckin' dinosaur."

I was speechless as Joe went on. "He swam right at me. But I put a damper on his fuckin' day."

"A damper how, exactly?" I wanted to ask, but Joe was already moving on. "With your paddle, or like a gun? Did you bring a gun, Joe? Should I have brought a gun, Joe? Fuck. *Do I need a fuckin' gun, Joe?*"

These things went unanswered. No one mentioned whether or not guns were a requirement in the brochure. The only means of protection I had on me was a spritz of bug spray.

As I paddled after Joe, I thought about all the childhood books I read on dinosaurs. They were cool in theory, sure, but I didn't actually care to *see* one. I felt completely satisfied by *Our Planet* documentaries narrated by Morgan Freeman. Even David Attenborough films about present-day reptiles were enough for me. I felt quite comfortable knowing that whatever few didn't go extinct lived somewhere in Zimbabwe. If a lifetime passed without ever crossing paths with something capable of a "death roll," well, that would have been just fine with me. Especially since the only other thing on the menu was largemouth bass. And let me ask you something about that: Have you ever seen largemouth bass being served at a restaurant? (Besides maybe in some bumblefuck town in Louisiana?) Of course you haven't.

There's a *reason* for that. Because they taste like mud. You know what probably doesn't taste like mud? Me—pickled by whatever gourmet meals I'd been fattening up with prior to venturing out into this murk, probably sweating garlic and thyme as I paddled after Joe.

For a man twice my age, his kayak sailed those waters more swiftly than mine. He was parked on a bank already hooking a rubber worm on the end of his line by the time I finally pulled up. Without removing his eyes from the task, he began to explain what I was to do: cast into pockets where bass may lurk and then reel the worm quickly so it left a rippling stream on the surface.

With this, he flicked his rod in demonstration with the finesse only a master angler could, dropping his worm into a hole in the grass I hadn't even seen. Immediately it felt like one of those unexplainable skills that only seasoned dads possess, which sons can strive for but never achieve. The worm hit the pocket and came rippling back toward us. Mere seconds passed before there was an explosion of water and the bait disappeared. Joe gave the rod a yank, and it curled over twitching. He reeled frantically as the line moved closer in the water. A moment or two later, a footlong bass breached the surface, flopping about wildly before splashing back into the drink. Joe reeled the line all the way to the boat and, just as he was about to lift the fish aboard, there was another spray of water and the rod snapped straight as the fish spat the hook free.

"Dammit!" I said.

"Easy come, easy go," said Joe, all too coolly. "Come on. Let's find a better spot."

A better spot? I thought. *We're one-for-one here. We're batting a thousand. How much better can it be?* But I had no time to argue. Joe was already paddling away.

I struggled to keep close behind as he cruised along, but I was within view when I saw his head snap to the side and one hand flail before his face as if to swat something away. A second later there was a splash in the water beside him.

"Son of a bitch!" he cried.

"What happened?" I yelled ahead.

"Bastard jumped up and hit me in the mouth."

"What did?"

"A fish."

"A fish *jumped* out of the water and hit you in the *mouth*?" I said.

"Yeah," he laughed. "Sometimes things get busy back here, but I've never had *that* happen."

Busy? I thought. *What is happening right now? Where are we?* In all my years of fishing up north, not once has a bass ever jumped out of the water to assault me.

Joe paddled on.

As I followed him along the narrow channel, I bumped into a patch of grass and there was a hasty rustling that scurried up the bank. Whatever it was must have been as spooked as I was because it moved too quickly to catch a glimpse. Joe was stopped ahead, looking back to make sure I was keeping up, and noticed me bump into the grass.

"Took a buddy back here once," he said. "Did somethin' just like that and a six-foot gator jumped out of the grass and ran right across his lap into the water."

I said nothing. I mean, what do you say to that?

Joe paddled on.

A short while later, he stopped again and waited. I pulled up next to him, and this time he took my pole from its holster and hooked a rubber worm on the end for me. He handed the rod back and said, "Why don't you cast right into that pocket over there and see what happens."

I snapped my rod in that direction, and as soon as I did, a gust of wind blew it right into the grass. How embarrassing. I gave it a quick jerk, and the worm came flying back in my direction, plunking down into the water next to me. How embarrassing.

"That's alright," said Joe. "Everyone does that sometimes." He, though, snapped his own rod into the intended pool easily. As I reeled up slack, he hooked another fish on the line. He reeled quickly, this time landing a two-pounder. With the ease that only comes from a thousand repetitions, he grabbed the bass by the lip with one hand and unhooked it with the other, barely acknowledging his success as he dropped it back in the water. Then he pushed off the shore with a casual, "Let's go."

Let's go? In the lakes and streams up north, you can fish for hours and not catch a thing. *This guy is two-for-two on casts and doesn't bat an eye! Let's go…*

But go we did, this time paddling for a longer stretch of stream. I was surprised to see another sign along the bank, this one reading *1.0 MILES*. The marker itself didn't surprise me, though; my arms were already tired.

The channel began to open a little wider as we approached a much larger pool off to the side, this one covered in lily pads. Joe slowed down and turned.

"Drop your line in there," he said. "That pool is full of bass."

I complied, flicking my worm toward the edge of the pads and began reeling.

Nothing.

Joe laughed. "I've never seen *that* before!" Then he cast his line way back onto the pads and began skipping his worm on and off the tops of them. It wasn't long before the bait was attacked by what looked like three different fish at once. On the last one, he went to set the hook too soon and the worm came flying back at him.

While he was reeling in his slack, I followed his lead by casting on top of the pads and began reeling. This time— *boom!*—an explosion of water and my line disappeared. I yanked the rod back to set the hook, and it curled over jiggling. I don't know what it is about that dancing tip of a rod that taps into something primal, but my guess is it's that I'll-be-able-to-feed-the-tribe-tonight tingle shooting through your DNA.

"Now you're gettin' the hang of it!" yelled Joe. But as soon as he did the rod snapped straight and the worm came shooting skyward.

"Easy come, easy go," I told him.

We paddled on.

We went deep into the area where the channel turned into an open swamp comprised of lily pad crops, islands of grass, and a maze of various water channels. Joe led me through it, casting into various pockets from time to time, pulling out fish here and there as we moved along.

It was fishing like I'd never seen. He told me he comes out here on long days with his son where they've hooked hundreds of bass. At times, his boy complained of boredom, asking how many fish they needed to catch. "All of 'em," Joe would reply. He was a true diehard.

When he told me the fishing here was an untapped secret, I asked him why no one else was out here.

"Lazy," was his short reply. "No one cares to put in the work."

I was looking around, appreciating the untouched beauty of such a secluded place, when I realized I had no idea where we were. In fact, I had no idea which direction civilization might be in at all. To the East—wherever that was—was a two-hour paddle to the boat launch. But to the West? One-and-a-half *million* acres of marshland riddled with gators and pythons of an unknown number.

"So," I asked, trying to push the thought aside, "you never see *any*one else back here?"

"In hundreds of trips," said Joe, "maybe even a thousand, the only person I've bumped into a couple of times is the game warden." Then he was courteous enough to share the story of a guy who'd ventured out here on his own one time and got turned around. Helicopters had to search for him. Unfortunately, Joe wasn't courteous enough to share how the story ended because he got distracted reeling in a huge bass.

I gulped. I gulped because this was when I realized I was truly alone with a man I'd just met somewhere in the middle of an uncharted swamp.

I don't know how far back we were exactly—miles of some lost count—but far enough where if I'd lost Joe (or, say, a bigger fish jumped out of the water and knocked him out cold), that would be the end of me. Far enough where if it came down to either spending the night paddling aimlessly around a bloodthirsty reptilian swamp or slitting my own throat with a pocket knife, it's a toss-up for what I would have chosen. Far enough where a modified version of that line from *Alien* might apply: "In the Everglades, no one can hear you scream." Like a child lured into a dark alley with the promise of candy, I'd been lured into a marshy abyss by the promise of largemouth bass.

The sun was going down; I felt it in my bones. It was beautiful, don't get me wrong—with the grassy shadows growing longer and a rustling breeze cooling the air—but it came with the realization that soon there wouldn't be a single light around. If there was a New Moon, for example, or a cloudy sky, the only flickering illumination might come from lightning bugs. Do the Everglades even have lightning bugs? Were they bloodthirsty too? What the fuck did I know. All I knew is the prospect of being a sitting duck in the middle of a nocturnal predator's playground seemed terrifying. It's an alligator's world, you know; we're just livin' in it.

"Cast over here," Joe called. I paddled close and parked in front of a pool of giant lily pads. "This is one of my favorite spots." He wasn't kidding. We pulled fish after fish out of that pool, including Joe landing one of the biggest bass I'd ever seen in my life. The thing must've weighed five or six pounds, twenty inches long, mouth the size of a softball. Joe dropped it back in the water casually without the slightest consideration of a photo before saying, "It's a shame the fishing's so slow."

"*Slow*?" I said.

"Oh, this is nothing," said Joe.

"Do you typically catch *two* giant bass per cast?" I asked. His math scrambled my brain.

"In another week, the females will be off the beds and starving," he replied. "Every cast will look like the one I just put back, or bigger."

My mind was so boggled that I fumbled with my reel, and the line dropped into the water next to the boat. As soon as it hit the surface, there was an explosion so loud it scared me.

"Jesus!" I yelled. But as I pulled my line out of the water, there was nothing. Just for kicks, though, I dropped it back in the same spot, and the same thing happened, this time my rod bent over harder than it had all day. I can't even claim I "reeled in" one of the biggest bass of my life. It wasn't even fair. I didn't even earn it. I didn't even want it that way. But there she was: a plump and pregnant female almost as big as Joe's.

"This is insane," I told him, setting her back into the water gently.

Joe laughed. "Isn't it, though?" Then he picked up his paddle and said, "Come on, I think I know a short cut back to the channel."

The words "I think" didn't inspire much confidence, but what the hell: as long as I was at risk of being stranded and eaten alive by bugs and reptiles, I may as well chance shaving off a few miles. Besides, dark was really creeping in now and I had no idea how long it would take us to get back to the boat launch.

I couldn't have asked for a better last sunset, though: pink-stricken clouds across a fading blue sky, the sun dipping behind the grass and whatnot. It was lovely. The "shortcut," on the other hand, turned out to be a huge pain in the ass. A lack of rain had left this portion of the Everglades low on water, and "paddling" through the sludge was tough. Instead, we stood like Venetian gondoliers, stabbing our oars into the muck to propel our boats forward. I don't know if "grueling" is the right word, but we certainly had our work cut out for us, and my arms were feeling it harder now.

Joe, however, seemed to thrive in the goop. As he sped along, I fell behind. He'd disappear around a bend, and I'd never know if I'd see him again. My heart would dance as I'd stab the muck with a little more ferocity until he appeared once more. I was dazedly following the faint trail his boat made in the swampy vegetation when all of a sudden there was an enormous lashing about mere inches from my kayak. A chaotic splashing of water went shooting away from me and disappeared somewhere into the swamp as I nearly shit my pants and fell into the muck at the same time. As I caught my balance, heart racing, I looked up to see Joe looking back at me laughing.

"If he was over ten feet, I would have warned ya!" he called back all amused.

I said nothing. I mean what do you say to that.

Joe paddled on.

We finally made it back to the channel and could float once more so I sat again. At this point the sun was down. Only the residual light of the day remained, but Joe insisted on a few more casts.

Paddle, cast. Paddle, cast. Paddle, cast. We crept our way back toward land as darkness swallowed the light. At one point he stopped for five minutes to tell a story and I wondered, *Does this guy have night vision goggles or something? Is he not concerned about being blind out here?*

Eventually he retired the rods, though, and we cruised along. But every so often he'd stop to point out the silhouette of a bird and say, "You see that?"

"No," I'd reply, squinting at the darkness.

"That's a rare glimpse of an Everglades sandpiper. One of them yuppy birdwatchers would kill to see that thing."

They'd have to die to see it first, I thought, something rustling through the grass and plunging into the water nearby.

Paddle, paddle, paddle. "That's a Wood Stork over there."

"Uh-huh," I'd say, thinking, *Birds are nice and all, Joe, but I'd rather keep all my limbs if you don't mind*, snapping around at another unseen splash in the river behind me.

At this point, it was really dark. To make things worse, a rumble of thunder roared in the distance, then a flash of lightning over the horizon. I think Joe sensed we were still quite a bit from shore because he began paddling like a madman. I mean, he was moving like he was trying to lose me; like this was SEALs training and I was some grunt being tested; like if I fell behind and was eaten by wildlife then, oh well, he'd just chalk my kayak up to a loss and move on.

I was sore, hungry, thirsty, scared, and could barely see, but I was also weighing my options: take a break to fall behind and most certainly be eaten, paddle slower to fall behind and likely be eaten, or push these thoughts out of my mind to paddle faster and hope not to get eaten. That's when I squinted into the dark to see we'd only just hit the *1.0 MILES* marker. I realized then just how big this gator-infested world is when you're at the mercy of your own manpower in a race against fading sunlight.

The motivation of either avoiding an untimely death or not looking like a pussy allowed me to dig deeper and tap into a new gear. I got up from my seat, squatted on my knees for leverage, and then pushed and pushed until I finally made up some ground on Joe.

At this point, either the wake of two boats was causing fish to jump wildly out of the water, or the gators were lurking underneath us at feeding time. I tried not to think of it either way and just ignored whatever splashes were happening in the dark around me.

Winged... *things* began swooping down across the path or flapping by my ear. They could have been those sight-of-a-lifetime storks the birdwatchers would kill to see, or they could have been pterodactyls for all my fight-or-flight system knew, but the internal reaction was the same: fear, fueling my already tired arms to paddle a little bit harder.

Joe stopped paddling all of a sudden and I caught up to him.

"You feel that?" he asked.

"Feel what?"

"We just ran over an eight-foot gator."

I said nothing. I mean what do you say to that.

"Just make sure to follow behind me," said Joe.

Then Joe paddled on.

On the outside I tried to project the kind of silent confidence Joe might expect from one of his fellow marines. That is, until I drifted a bit wide of Joe's trail and a sudden thrashing smacked against my bow and sent a jolt of panic up my spine. I let out a squeamish gasp as the slithering wake of a reptile went shooting off into deeper waters.

"What happened?" said Joe, turning around.

"G-g-g-gator!" I squeaked.

"You didn't see him? I told you to follow me. Why do you think I veered to the right?"

Joe turned back. Joe paddled on. Joe began fading into the night while I swallowed my pride through a very parched throat.

I went to sit back down from my kneeling position, but as I plopped into my seat, something slimy wriggled beneath my ass and then stung me. I jumped up and almost tipped my kayak into the river. "Fuck!" I screamed. I turned to find a bluegill with its dorsal spines extended, now flopping around the kayak. I tried to grab it carefully without getting stabbed again, but it already alluded my grasp for more of head start than I wanted to give Joe. Eventually I used the paddle as a giant scoop and flung it onto the bank to be eaten by whatever was rustling around over there. I thought I heard the *snap, snap, snap* of gator-chomping justice, but maybe it was just wishful thinking that karma got that little fucker.

I paddled on.

Mosquitos and horseflies began their attack. My spritz of five star rated bug repellent did nothing to stop those pests. (Thanks for nothing, Amazon reviewers. Bunch of weekend warriors in your suburban backyards.)

Finally—*finally!*—what appeared to be the pale glow of the open water at the boat launch appeared in the distance. Fatigue was behind me now. The adrenaline was pumping and I paddled like I felt: as though I wanted to get the hell out of this Godforsaken swamp.

It was, indeed, land ho! We crushed the last 100m like Olympic racers and slid right up into the sand. I didn't get out and kiss the ground in front of Joe, but I did say a silent prayer. At least I began to when Joe pointed across the channel and said, "That's a *big* fucker there."

Sure enough, in the early reflections of moonlight, calmly gliding across the channel we had just paddled through, was the silhouette of a gator as long as our kayaks.

"I'd like to introduce *him* to Mr. Rogers," said Joe.

"Mr. Rogers?" I asked.

"My gun," said Joe.

I said nothing. I mean…

The constellations glowed over us as we packed the kayaks into the truck and eventually pulled away. Before we left the boat launch, though, Joe parked his truck right at the water's edge and turned his high beams on.

"You see all those little red reflections?"

"Yeah," I said, "of course," seeing what looked like a high school teenager's face dotted with acne.

"Gators' eyes," said Joe.

"Are you shitting me!? And we were just paddling in there?"

"Yeah, there's no shortage of 'em out here."

And so, what I mean to tell you, dear reader, is that the ending of this story could have gone many ways. Instead of this first-hand account, who knows what guesswork you might have read in the papers by the detectives assigned to the case. My floating corpse could have been run over randomly by the game warden, found strangled and pumped full of a militiaman's semen. Or I could have been pinned to the ground by my ballsack and left to squeal like a little piggy, this time with no arrow coming to put an end to the ordeal. Or I could have disappeared from the face of the earth altogether, literally swallowed by nature. And, as with the emotionless current of those waters, the world would have flowed on without me.

But the fact is that the ending of this cautionary tale is none of those. Instead, on the way home, Joe bought me pizza, and now we're friends.

SCOUTING WITH JOE

"More people are killed every year by pigs than by sharks,
which shows you how good we are at evaluating risk."
—*Bruce Schneier*

"Yeah," Joe scoffed. "They even fined a little boy. They're absolute assholes down here." He was telling me about a ticket he'd received for parking in the Wildlife Management Area we were entering now. "We don't need to pay that," said Joe, blowing by a sign that read $3 PER PERSON OR $6 PER VEHICLE. "I've already got my pass." I chuckled at the fuck-you attitude with which he sped past the nominal fee.

We bumped our way down a dirt road that eventually opened up to a parking lot. There were signs posted everywhere that made it clear the lot was for hikers only, *not* hunters. Joe pulled to the side and turned off the truck as he said, "This is where I parked when that cocksucker wrote me a ticket. I've been parking here for thirty years without a problem before those signs went up. The only reason they're here is because every one of us who got fined went down to the courthouse to fight it."

We put on our packs and locked up the truck before Joe led me down an overgrown path. "Every one of us," said Joe, "one-by-one, went up to that judge and showed her pictures how there were no signs, and showed proof that this was the designated area for the season. And every one of us, one-by-one, got our cases dismissed in front of that asshole. That poor little kid was so traumatized he could barely speak to the judge. His father told her that if he ever saw that officer again, he'd rip his fuckin' head off. And I believed him, too. He was a big motherfucker. You shoulda seen the look on that officer's face when he said that. Serves him right, though. They are real pieces of shit down here. Every one of 'em."

It was ninety-five degrees; one of those humid Florida days where you're drenched in sweat the minute you step out of the car and there's nothing you can do about it. As we walked down the trail, Joe pointed to various imprints in the mud and said "raccoon" or "deer" or "turkey." Once he stopped and pointed to a grasshopper three times the size of what I'm used to up north, painted yellow the likes of which I've never seen. Joe bent down and pinched its legs together so he could pick it up. The thing didn't even try to hop away, like it knew if it resisted there'd be trouble from Joe. After giving me a closer look at what I thought should be reported as a species discovery, Joe tossed it aside like an apple core and marched on.

He stopped a little further down the path and pointed to a swampy opening and said, "That's what hogs do." An area the size of a small house had been rooted up and turned over for all the plant life to die. "They're a real problem down here," said Joe.

"Jeez," I said. "That's huge!"

"That's nothing," said Joe. Then he turned and marched on.

Later, I found that hogs were brought to the States in the 1500s by settlers. Free-range livestock and escapees from enclosures led to the establishment of feral swine. If you saw a map of where they roamed in America in 1982, you might not think their presence in a few parts of the south was such a big deal. But if you saw how far their range has exploded in the last couple of decades, reaching as far north as the Great Lakes, you'd think they're spreading like a virus—which is fitting considering they're known to carry at least thirty different kinds, all of which can be transmitted to humans, pets, and livestock. What's a conservative estimate of the damage they cause to farms and the environment, you ask? Ohh, around $1.5 *billion* a year or so.

"They'll even attack little children in their own backyards," said Joe, spitting a stream of dip spit with that classic *pwtt* sound dip-spitters make. I did a search to confirm this later and found a recent tale of a woman in Texas whose corpse was found being gnawed on by hogs. They only ate her legs, though, so at least they're courteous enough to consider an open casket.

As we marched on, Joe would point up, down, left, or right and say things like, "Watch out for those." Once he pointed to an innocent-looking spider and told me, "If that thing bites you, it'll feel like acid's burning through your skin."

"Great," I said, gooseflesh bubbling up my arms.

On another occasion, Joe pointed to a vine with leaves on it and said, "Don't touch that."

"What is it?" I asked

"Poison [something or another]," said Joe.

I thought to myself, *But it looks like everything else out here...*

Joe knows his surroundings. I am not Joe.

At one point we stepped off the main trail into a mud pit and started walking deep into the woods. Joe pointed all around at mud wallows and uprooted plants and said, "That's what hogs do." I was amazed at the destruction they cause.

More and more puddles began to appear. At first, I tried to tip-toe around them, but I noticed Joe splashing right through them. I looked at the boots on his feet and they appeared to be knee-high waterproof hunting boots, designed for this sort of thing. I looked down at the worn-out ankle-high hiking boots on my own feet, not designed for this sort of thing. Eventually, the ground became one big puddle and tiptoeing was a lost cause. At that point, the water poured in and filled my socks till they *squish*ed.

Joe came prepared. I am not Joe.

Eventually the woods opened up into a grassy swamp of shin-deep water with islands of land peppered around. "Stay away from those," said Joe, pointing to a nearby patch of flowers in the water. "They only grow over bottomless holes."

I laughed. I'm not even sure why.

"You think I'm kidding?" said Joe. "I swear they're ten feet deep."

"You know from experience?" I asked.

Joe nodded. Joe *pwtt*. Joe marched on.

As we wandered around, Joe pointed out various game trails and said, "Come hunting season, this whole place will be covered in those."

"Why do they wait for hunting season?" I asked.

Joe said, "When rifle areas open, they'll come charging in here like a stampede to hide. No one ever hunts back here because it's archery-only, and no one likes the terrain."

I could see why. The woods on the islands were so thick we had to crouch down and push over branches to get through. To give you an idea, at one point Joe said, "If we want to hunt some of these islands, we're gonna have to come back with machetes."

Joe owns a machete. I am not Joe.

Florida swamp mosquitoes are a different breed. They are vicious, they are bloodthirsty, and they don't give a fuck about the bug repellent neck gaiter you bought from Amazon. They'll chew through that thing like vampires munch on babies. Joe has a neck so red my guess is it's charred beyond feeling pesky little skeeters like those. These are the virtues of being a redneck that I'd never known.

As we marched through the mud, Joe pointed down at a track the size of a jar and said, "Cat." As we marched through the sand, Joe pointed down at a track thrice the size and said, "Bear." As we marched through the grass, Joe pointed at something I didn't even see and said, "Snake." Bobcats and pythons and black bears, oh my...

Joe is unbothered. I am not Joe.

Joe led me through the branches of thick islands. As he went through first, they would swing back at me. If I followed closely, I could grab them before he let go. If I followed further back they would swing to rest before I got there. But in the Goldilocks zone, where the distance I followed was just right, when looking down at something I thought might be slithering through my feet, a branch would come swinging back and—*schwapp!*—hit me right in the face.

Ow.

These sounds became the beat to which we marched through swamp for hours.

Squish

Pwtt

Schwapp

Ow

Squish

Pwtt

Schwapp

Ow

"That's what hogs do," said Joe, pointing to another large wallow. "And they're tough little bastards. One time I was hunting on a buddy's farm with my son and shot one clean through the vitals. He ran off three hundred yards. We tracked him down and found him grunting wildly in a bush and I plugged another one in him. Then he got up and started charging me."

"He *charged* you?"

"Oh yeah," said Joe. "They'll charge right at you with their nasty little fangs and try to run you down. You have to jump out of the way before they getcha."

"Even after you shot him, *twice*?"

"I'm telling ya," said Joe, "they're tough bastards. This one ran off and disappeared over a hill. We blood trailed him and found him panting in a waterhole and came up with a plan. I gave my son a pistol and told him if he runs at him, plug one right between his eyes. Meanwhile, I snuck around and shot him again from forty yards. Sure enough, he came sprinting right at my son and—*bam!*—square in the forehead. But the fucker still didn't go down."

"You're kidding…"

"I'm not," said Joe. "He starts running in circles and squealing like mad so my son just unloaded on him. That put him down. We were guttin' the thing and my buddy came riding over the hill in a quad and said, 'What the fuck is going on back here!? It sounds like World War Three!'"

Joe laughed. I shook my head. We marched on.

We came to a patch of land that looked like every other patch of land and Joe said, "I call this Hog Island." Then he pointed overhead and told me, "Killed plenty from that tree right there. You'll see over two-hundred of 'em runnin' around come season."

"Two *hundred* hogs!?" I said. "I've never even seen *one*."

Joe ignored this embarrassing admission.

"How many hogs have you killed over the years?"

"No idea," said Joe.

"Take a wild guess."

He stopped and turned back at me as he said, "Let's put it this way. I shot a hundred and seventy-three in one year in the orange groves." Then he turned and marched on while I chewed on that for a while.

Joe's slaughtered an average of a pig every other day for a year. I am not Joe.

Joe got far enough ahead where a cat or a snake or a bear could've gotten between us so I hustled to catch him. As soon as I did, I began to ask about these orange groves and—*schwapp!*

Ow.

"They were causing problems up there and needed the population managed," said Joe. "So me and a couple buddies went up there and took care of it."

"What did you do with all that meat?" I asked.

"Donated it," said Joe.

Squish

Pwtt

Schwapp

Ow

Squish

Pwtt

Schwapp

Ow

"That's what hogs do," said Jo—

All the sudden there was siren going off somewhere in the distance and Joe stopped.

"You hear that?" he asked.

"Yeah, what is it?"

"Lightning detector," said Joe. And sure enough, as we marched through an open patch of swamp, a bolt of lightning streaked across the horizon.

"Sooo," I asked, "you feel comfortable sitting up in a tree during a storm?"

"I grew up in Florida," said Joe, swatting his hand the way you'd express That-doesn't-bother-me. "You get used to this kind of weather. If you start to feel static electricity, just lay on the ground and you'll be fine." He said it with so much confidence it almost made sense.

Joe is unconcerned. I am not—*schwapp!*

Squish

Pwtt

Schwapp

Ow

Squish

Pwtt

Schwapp

Ow

"You know what those are from?" said Joe, pointing to some grooves in the mud that appeared as though an anchor had been dragged through them.

"No idea."

"Gator tails," said Joe.

"Oh," I said, trying to sound cool. "I knew that."

Joe *pwtt.* I gulped. We marched on.

"I was up in that tree once," said Joe, pointing over us again, "and right around dusk this *enormous* gator, and I mean fuckin' *huge*, crawled right up under my tree and parked himself along the trail I was hunting. He had the same idea I did," said Joe, "but I didn't exactly wanna spook him in the dark when I had to climb down that night. So, you know what I did?"

"I've got a hun—"

"Shot him right in the fuckin' head—*bam!*"

"Can't say I blame y—"

"What was I supposed to do? I wasn't gonna climb down in the dark and ask if he was hungry."

Joe's killed monsters. I am not Joe. I *squish*ed behind Joe a little closer than before.

After we'd wandered for what felt like hours—weeks for all I knew—Joe pointed over yonder and said, "You know where we came from, right?"

I thought, *I haven't a clue where we came from*, but I said, "Of course I know where we came from."

Joe pointed toward an unseen canal the opposite way and said, "Well, now we're gonna have to kayak in from there since we can't park at my spot anymore."

Which means, I gathered, *we'll have to kayak out again, in the dark, with a tasty hog strapped to our boats.*

Squish

Pwtt

Schwapp

Ow

Squish

Pwtt

Schwapp

Ow

"Now what do you think made that?" said Joe, pointing to a mud wallow the size of a bathtub in the ground.

"A squirrel?" I said, trying to restrain a smile.

Joe cocked his head to the side and stared at me the way a militia man might stare at a civilian wiseguy.

Squish

Pwtt

Schwapp

Ow

As we found our way back to the main trail, we approached a boardwalk in the middle of the park. It was brand new construction, but about halfway along it there was a barricade where the new build stopped and the old boardwalk was unfinished on the other side.

"What's that sign say?" asked Joe.

When we got close enough to read *CLOSED FOR RENOVATIONS* I said, "Aw schucks, Joe. Would you look at that? Looks like we'll have to turn arou—"

Without breaking stride, Joe kicked one leg over the sign followed by the other and pushed forward. And so the rotting planks creaked beneath our feet as we marched on.

Squish

Creak

Squish

Pwtt

Squish

Creak

Squish

Pwtt

Eventually, we circled back to the parking lot and hopped in the truck. "There's one more place I wanna show you," said Joe. So, we drove back down the dirty road. We bumped along for a while before turning right down another road. As soon as we did, a game warden parked behind a line of trees, blared his siren, flashed his lights, and pulled out behind us.

As Joe stopped, he looked up at another new sign that read *ROAD CLOSED TO MOTOR VEHICLES.* "Ah, shit," he said. "What's this guy's problem? It's not like I drove past it yet."

The game warden got out of his truck and walked up to the window. "Where you boys going?" he said.

"I'm just showin' him around the park," said Joe, jerking a thumb my way. "But I see the sign says no vehicles, so I was about to turn around."

Without a breath of hesitation, the game warden said, "I'm still gonna write you a warning for not knowing where you're going. Do you have a management stamp on you?"

As Joe was getting out his wallet, the game warden asked me, "And you, son? You have your stamp on you?"

Before I could open my mouth, Joe said, "He just moved down here. I was just showing him around."

Before Joe finished speaking, the game warden said, "That's fine and all, Mr…" He paused to look at the ID Joe handed him and continued, "Hartland, but I was talking to him." Then he looked back at me.

"Like he said," I said. "I just moved down here. I don't even know what you're asking for."

A second game warden suddenly materialized outside my window like a ghost and said, "You have a driver's license, son?"

Startled, I snapped around and said, "Yeah, sure," and removed my wallet from my pocket to hand it over.

"Well," the first game warden said to Joe, "I'm gonna write you up that warning now. Then we'll figure out what to do with your *buddy* here." He turned to head back to his truck and said, "You two just sit tight."

And sit tight we did, as the game wardens did who the hell knows what inside their truck for twenty minutes.

"You look nervous," said Joe. "You don't have any warrants out for your arrest, do you?"

"No," I told him. "I'm not nervous, I just don't care for authority."

Although I've never been arrested, nor charged with a speeding ticket, nor anything else that might appear on my record, I've had a few unpleasant encounters with police in my youth pertaining to the oh-so-egregious crime of smoking a little pot as a teenager. Needless to say, I never cared for people who chose to use their badge to spend time harassing people who aren't bothering anyone when there are plenty of rapists, murderers, and poachers on the loose. The point is that Joe had a management stamp, and a VA card, and I am not Joe.

"Here you are, sir," said the first warden, appearing back on Joe's side. "Just a warning for you." Then he looked at me and said, "Son, would you step out of the vehicle please?" And so step out of the vehicle please I did.

I met him around the back of the truck as he asked, "Do you two have any weapons in the vehicle? Rifles? Bows? Anything like that?"

"No. Like we said, he was just showing me around."

"Son, it doesn't bother me if you were putting up trail cameras or what you were doing out there, but in order be in this part of the park, you need to have a day pass or a wildlife management stamp. This here," he said, handing me a clipboard with a sheet of paper and a pen, "is a citation for breaking the law."

"All we did was go on a hike," I said, "and he has a parking pass."

"Yes, son, *he* has a pass. But from what I understand, *you* don't possess a day pass or a wildlife management stamp, do you?"

"The sign at the entrance says you pay per vehicle," I said.

"That only covers direct family, son. Now, are *you* direct family?"

"No," I sighed, looking at the fine, "we're just friends."

"Now, signing this is not an admission of guilt, merely an acknowledgment that you received this fine. You can either pay those sixty dollars in the next thirty days, or, if you feel you've unjustly been issued this fine, you can set a date to fight it in court."

"Is there any chance of me actually disputing this?" I asked.

"I can't tell you that, son," said the warden. Then with a big and pompous smile he added, "But if you do, I'll be there to fight it."

I shook my head as I signed.

"Oh," he added, exuding a sense of unnecessary joy, "if you fail to do so, there will be a warrant out for your arrest."

"A warrant out for my arrest, for taking a hike in a state park," I said, handing him back the clipboard. "Noted."

As I *squish*ed back to the truck, wondering how people like that live with themselves, he told me to have a splendid day.

Joe got off with a warning. I am definitely, positively not Joe.

"What did I tell you?" said Joe, firing up the truck before we bounced down the road. "They're absolute shitheads in Florida. I've never met a single one who wasn't an asshole down here. Even the people I knew that became cops turned into assholes." When I remained silent, he said, "I'm really sorry about that. Just pay it. It's not worth the trouble. And if it's about the money, I'll pay it for you."

It wasn't about the money. It was the principle of the matter.

The next day, I looked up the rule he fined me for and found that it contradicted what I was being fined for. I was furious. I wanted to call and report this asshole to his boss. I had my speech prepared. ("Which part of 'serve and protect' does this fall under exactly? Is this the kind of scum you allow to carry around a lethal weapon?") But instead, I spent the next three days calling six different numbers, going through one of those mazes organizations set up to discourage you from actually contacting them. I was transferred a dozen times to a dozen different dispatchers in a dozen different offices. Not one of them had a clue about the rules pertaining to state parks. I left voicemails, I collected extension numbers, I had my information "taken down" and "passed along."

On one phone call, after being transferred to a transfer from a transferred transfer, I asked the woman, "What are the chances I'll be transferred to someone who understands whether or not I'm allowed to hike in the state parks my taxes pay for before a warrant goes out for my arrest?"

"Son, I don't have that answer for you," she told me, "but I'd be happy to transfer you."

With a defeated sigh, I told her that'd be great, thank you.

I was eventually transferred to a woman who seemed to have a grasp on who to transfer me to. She told me, "I'd be happy to transfer you to the officer who wrote you the citation?"

I said, "And what good would that do me exactly?"

She didn't have a response to that, but she made sure to take down my information so she could pass it along.

An hour later, my phone actually rang and I fumbled and almost dropped it, I was so caught off guard.

"Hello!? Lieutenant? Yes, it's me, the unjustly punished citizen who called pertaining to your abusive officer."

"Hello, son," said the woman who passed along my information. "I've passed along your information, but I've been instructed to tell you that if you feel like you've been unjustly given a ticket, you can always appear in court and dis—"

A blood vessel popped somewhere in my brain as I said, "Yes, I *know* that, thank you. It says it right on the ticket and I possess this rare trait called literacy. I'm calling to speak to the boss of the guy who issued the ticket."

"Very good then, son," she said. "I've taken down your information and passed it along."

An hour later the phone rang again.

"Hello..?"

"Yes, this is Lieutenant Asshole," a voice introduced themselves. "I've been passed along some information t pertaining to a law you violated."

"Yes! Well, no…" I fumbled over his trickery of words. "I'd just like some clarification on this rule here."

"Yes, son, you were in violation of rule 68A-15.004, General Regulations Relating to Wildlife Management Areas. What seems to be the problem?"

"Well, it says here on my ticket, 'A short-term use permit is mandatory on those wildlife management areas where required by regulations for that area.' But the *full* rule online goes on to say that 'a non-permitted individual may accompany a permittee but shall not occupy a vehicle separate from the permittee.'"

"And what seems to be the problem?"

"I was in the same vehicle as a permittee."

"Son, upon entering the park, there is a clear sign stating you need to buy a daily permit."

"Yes, it also says you can pay per vehicle."

With a heavy sigh and growing aggravation, he said something like, "Son, it's clearly posted in fine print on a board no one would ever see, buried under a bunch of other posts tacked on top of it, and probably rained out because it's so old, that if you're not a *direct* relative of the owner of the vehicle, you need to purchase a day pass for yourself. That's why we make the information so readily available to the public. Now, are you the vehicle owner's son or spouse?"

"No, what? We're just fr—"

"Well then, son, as I'm not a lawyer, I'm not allowed to give you any legal advice. But I suggest if you still feel you've been unjustly issued the citation, you set yourself a date in court and dispute it. Now is there anything else I can help you with before I get on with my life's work of fucking other people over the same way we just fucked you?"

"Well, um… No, I guess not then," I said.

"Then you have yourself a splendid day, you fuckin' loser. And if you ever dare bother me about something like this again, I'll put a warrant out for your arrest for that too. Do I make myself clear?"

"Yes, sir. Thank you, si—"

Click.

In the end, I did not get my ticket overturned in court. Instead, I ended up mailing in a check for sixty dollars because apparently, these people have never heard of the internet, so I couldn't even pay online. I'm not even sure if they ever received it because I never received any confirmation. For all I know, there could be a warrant out for my arrest right now. But if there's one thing I do know, it's that I am definitely, positively, absolutely not Joe.

Two weeks later, though, Joe relayed a story told to him by one of his police officer pals. Apparently, the same game warden who wrote me that ticket had sand thrown in his face before being kicked in the balls by a couple of Vietnamese old-timers he failed to catch stealing sea turtle eggs from the beach. Nothing against turtles, but a couple of reptiles is a price I'm willing to pay for justice. And while I do believe an eye for an eye can make the whole world blind, I also think an eye for a swift kick in the balls could rid the world of fertile jerks, wouldn't you agree?

HUNTING WITH JOE

"The history of the bow and arrow
is the history of mankind."
—Fred Bear

Dragging a body through the Everglades is no easy task. Months—even years—of physical preparation leading up to it won't prepare you for the task. There are no trails; it's just brush and mud and palmettos and thoughts of, *Oh my God. Was that an alligator growling?* Not to mention it's almost 100 degrees with almost 100% humidity, and dark. The easiest part is trudging through grassy stretches of knee-deep water, but even then, you're open game for countless species of mosquitoes, some the size of half-dollars. But that's what it takes to kill in Florida.

I remember the first time I took a life. God, she was beautiful. It wasn't easy. I was nervous, full of hesitation, adrenaline pumping through my veins. The thousands of arrows I'd shot into stationary, lifeless targets did nothing to prepare me for that moment. All those instances of hitting the bullseye failed me when this creeping target made a move I wasn't prepared for. I hit her shoulder and she dropped to the ground, but from the loud cry and flopping around, I immediately knew what I *hadn't* done.

From where I was perched, though, I no longer had a clear second shot with where she landed. I climbed down from the tree as quickly as I could and slowly approached her. The look of terror in her eyes when she saw me coming and tried to flop away was horrible. I wanted to end it as quickly for her as I did for myself, so I nocked another arrow and took aim as I released at point-blank range into her ribcage. I'll never forget the sound of air squealing out of her lungs as I stepped away to give her space to die.

As I walked backward and behind her, she rolled her neck over to stare at me as she expired, with eyes that pleaded, *Why!?* It was heartbreaking, but I forced myself not to look away. I was either going to be too traumatized to eat meat ever again, or I was going to accept my hand in the circle of life and embrace a lifestyle of being intimately connected with my food. When I finally walked back after she was gone, I was flooded with a combination of sadness, relief, gratitude, and some kind of primal satisfaction that I'd never felt before.

You see photos of these almost mythic beings in magazines, or perhaps you even catch a glimpse of them as they dart across the road, but mostly they evade the human eye. To touch one for the first time was surreal, spiritual even. Knowing that I'd feed myself, my family, and my friends for many meals, all due to the consequence of my own intentional actions, was something I hesitate to call special.

How many countless times has a waitress dropped off a cheeseburger, a steak, or a meat lover's pizza while I coughed up a half-sincere, "Thanks." Every meal I'd eaten prior was immediately made meaningless in comparison to personally taking a life that would soon feed myself and others. Reflecting on all the hours at the range, reps in the gym, miles of hiking, money spent on gear, all welled up inside of me as I stroked the silky neck of this fallen being. I'm not ashamed to admit a tear or two streamed down my cheeks at that point. That moment became one of, if not the most, significant of my life.

It felt *real*. School, work, sports, partying: they all immediately became overshadowed in an instant by this experience. *This is real*, is all I kept thinking. It was the first time I felt a part of the ecosystem, like I'd finally stepped into the circle of natural existence. I thanked her repeatedly for giving her life in exchange for the life she'd be providing me, my friends, and my family.

A lot of life skills, life lessons, and life-long friends have come from hunting. Learning to butcher, process, and cook wild game is among the most obvious. The community built around like-minded living is another perk of the trade. But there are more subtle benefits to this lifestyle that aren't as readily apparent.

For example, the simple pleasure of inhaling the aroma from a cabin woodstove after being humbled by frigid winter temps for hours (hunting outside of Florida, that is). Or seeing things you wouldn't normally see—like raccoons, or coyotes, or bobcats, or a hawk snatch two baby squirrels from the same nest on two separate occasions as momma squirrel cries out in anguish. (What a front-row seat into the brutality of nature *that* was.)

Another example is experiencing this moment in the woods that is my favorite time of day. It's the small window of time when night ends and day begins. It's when the first shy hint of light begins to illuminate the woods, but only enough to see the world in shades of gray. It's the moment the world feels still, as if it's stopped moving altogether. Everything that was awake at night has gone to rest, while everything that lives in the light is yet to rise. It's this moment of utter silence that doesn't last long. And it's in this moment that you can't help but feel at peace.

Then the first bird breaks the silence—*cheep-cheep, cheep-cheep*. Then another chimes in. Then another, and the silence is gone. The chipmunks and squirrels begin scurrying about in the leaves, and the distant sounds of humans end any remanence of quiet as well. For me, that moment makes waking up long before the sunrise all worthwhile.

Being alone with your thoughts in nature for hours is another less obvious benefit of hunting. As exciting and emotionally charged as the moments of action can be, most of hunting is just, well, waiting. When alone in the woods without distraction for hours, with the elements and hunger testing your mind, it becomes difficult to stuff your formally suppressed feelings down, to drink them away, or turn on a ballgame instead of facing what's emerging. But in the woods, there is none of that. There is you and your mind, alone together. Consciousness strays into the realm of weird curiosities about life, or remembrances of strange times in the past. I'll let your imagination fill in the blank of what might surface when undistracted for so long, but I've been out in the middle of nowhere processing things I never saw coming.

Then, you may be in the middle of this deep contemplation when all of a sudden you're interrupted by the *slosh, slosh, slosh* of swampy footsteps that you can hear before you can see. Your mind snaps back to the task at hand and sometimes you're faced with a few-second window to judge the legality of horns before pulling back your bow to release. The moment you've been anticipating for months might be over before it started, your body reacting through instincts woven into your system by the hundreds of arrows shot in the months leading up to this.

On this particular occasion, perched in a palm tree just a hundred yards from Joe, my first eight-point buck appeared in a window small enough where any hesitation would have led to a missed opportunity. And had I missed that opportunity, I would have blown the only chance I'd have all year.

Sometimes, it's like that, depending on your schedule, land access, and the particular season for the area you're hunting. It was a very uneventful season for me after opening day, but fortunately, I didn't miss the one chance I had that year. That eight-point rack now stares at me from the bookshelf next to my pull-up bar, reminding me why I need to keep in shape for days like those. The only motivation I need is the reminder about the drudgery of dragging a body through the Everglades.

That said, hunting is possibly the only sport where all the preparation in the world can still yield nothing, all because you're at the mercy of Lady Luck. She alone decides what may or may not cross your path. Sometimes you see nothing as it rains for hours, and all you get is soaked. But if you're patient and persistent enough to show up time and time again, sometimes—*sometimes*—your luck may just turn around.

AN ELEGY FOR ESTHER

"You have a gift. Stick with it."
—The man at Grandma's funeral who gave me an inspirational
shake of the hand after this piece had been read aloud.

The following was originally a post I made on my grandmother's Facebook page after she died. To my surprise, my father passed it along to the minister in charge of her service to be read aloud. I include it here both as a way to dedicate this book to her, but also to the nameless, faceless man who helped spark my inspiration to take writing more seriously.

Grandma,

You always loved and supported my writing, so here's one last piece for you:

A is for Air cookies, which I've probably drooled over my last of due to the near impossible conditions and personal touch required to produce such delectable morsels of goodness.

B is for the weeklong "Beach-cations" we took every year as a family from the time we were babies through young adulthood. Those times were true blessings and shaped my love for so many things that they brought along with them.

C is for the Camp Woodruff that built a tight bond between cousins spending annual week-long visits at your house, delicately balanced between pampering and chores.

D is for Daisy—the Crazy kind, that is. That, oh so wild, sprinkler system kept us "ankle-biters" occupied and cool in the thick and stagnant summer heat of central Connecticut.

E is for English, which I owe you a great deal for enlightening me to the difference between "William and I" versus "Me and William" (which could easily be confused for "Mean William," which he's not).

F is for the countless hours of Frisbee tossed around your backyard. I wouldn't trade anything for the laughs and joyous moments spent on your expansive, grassy lawn year after year.

G is for the Gummies—in the form of blue and white sharks or colorful worms—awarded to children for good behavior during Misquamicut vacations.

H is for "Hot Now!" and my first bite of a fresh Krispy Kreme donut, which took place under your roof at Worthington Ridge.

I is for the Iced Tea & Lemonade mix—your refreshing, summery drink served in those blue, plastic glasses that could quench any thirst in the heat of your family barbecues.

J is for the shape caterpillars make as they hang before turning into a chrysalis. Which I feel is also a metaphor for the phase of life you helped all of your grandchildren grow through. I know we'll all continue on through our metamorphosis just like the countless other butterflies you helped bring into this world.

K is for, "The Kitchen is closed!" The lovingly stern expression snapped at any post dinner remarks about lingering hunger pangs.

L is for the unconditional Love given to anyone who crossed your path, and the Love they couldn't help but to feel for you in return because of your magnificent demeanor and charm.

M is for the steamy summer days spent at Memorial Pool, where the concrete was hot enough to burn your feet, and each grandchild was given their dollar to spend on one candy treat.

N is for "Ne fais pas ça!," your French expression meaning, "Do not do that!," heard all too often growing up in swarm of delinquent grandchildren.

O is for Omelets, or Grandmomelets, as I preferred to call the fluffiest serving of piping hot breakfast one could enjoy.

P is for Point-and-Pull, the "game" that, to the untrained eye, could be mistaken for child slave labor on hot summer days spent removing an infestation of Japanese Bamboo, one Willis umbrella point at a time.

Q is for the Quality family time spent playing cards, watching movies, hosting picnics, cooking dinners, sharing gifts, and gathering around the magic candle.

R is for Remembering to take photos on every family occasion. As much as we resisted posing for those childhood photos, you knew how valuable the memories would be when they appeared in your family calendar at Christmas every year.

S is for the Stuffed Animal you bought me on the day of my birth, which I've kept to this day. I'll cherish it forever in loving memory of you.

T is for Teacher. Teacher of third-grade. Teacher of English. Teacher of positivity. Teacher of love and kindness. Teacher of many life lessons. And, perhaps most importantly, Teacher of Canasta.

U is for the many afternoons spent lounged in a circle Under the shade of your enormous trees, talking, napping, snacking, crossword puzzling, or just enjoying the breeze and good company.

V is for Valerie, Charlie, William, Anna, Nathan, David, Ryan, Ben, and Seth. A close-knit group of family members I couldn't imagine having grown up without. Pieces of you will live on in each of your grandchildren.

W is for Willis, who many of us wouldn't be here without. The man who brought you from Florida to start this amazing family. The man who sat me on his lap and introduced me to stories like *The Three Little Pigs*. The man I wish I could have been old enough to play *Pente* and croquet with. But, most importantly, the man I owe so much to, for I can continue to enjoy everything you two left behind.

X is a (useless!) letter in whose place I'll put another 'M' for Monarchs and "The Butterfly Lady" who brought joy to countless others with her collection and display of the life cycle of the Monarch Butterfly. It was a sorrowful inevitability that your own life cycle had to end, but I feel blessed I was able to spend as much time in your presence as I did.

Z is for the Zoo you'd take us to during Camp Woodruff. I'll never forget the first time I stared through a thin layer of glass, deep into the eyes of an owl, or discovered the indescribable softness of a chinchilla. Those times spent with you are some of my most cherished and vivid childhood memories.

and, lastly,

Y is for, "You take care of yourself now," which were the last words you spoke to me before I heard the final click of your classic, black house phone. You were caring and thoughtful even through the final twenty-four hours of life. I couldn't have asked for a more peaceful ending to our loving relationship.

I'll have to apologize for any grammatical errors, but my primary proofreader has left my side. Thank you for everything, Grandma. I wouldn't be who I am without you. I'm not ashamed to admit I shed more than one tear recalling these memories of you. I miss you already, but you'll be forever cherished in my heart. May your beautiful soul Rest In Peace.

An endless amount of love and gratitude,
Kyle

CLOSING REMARKS

Thanks for bearing with me through all those stories. I know things got a little personal toward the end there. I'm sure you learned a thing or two about me that you could have gone without.

TMI? Whoops.

But seriously, cleanse your colon.

I'd also like to thank all of life's characters who inspired these stories, as well as anyone who helped me critique my writing throughout the process. This book obviously wouldn't exist without them.

And if at any point you were offended, my dear reader, well, then, I just want to say, from the bottom of my heart, that I'd like to take this chance to apologize (in the voice of Conor McGregor) *to absolutely nobody!* Because I think perhaps you, too, deserve a good SUTH.

If you weren't, however, and you wouldn't mind helping a fella out with a quick rating or review, it would be greatly appreciated:

www.ingramcontent.com/pod-product-compliance
Lightning Source LLC
Chambersburg PA
CBHW060743050426
42449CB00008B/1291